BEST OF

# CHICKEN

GARDEN of GRAPES.



Printed in the USA.

# Introduction

Ladies and gentlemen, fellow food explorers, welcome to a culinary journey that's all about embracing the humble hero of our kitchens - the chicken. As you crack open these pages, get ready to embark on a global adventure that'll have your taste buds soaring and your kitchen sizzling.

First things first, let me extend a warm welcome, a virtual handshake if you will, as we dive headfirst into "Best of Chicken." This isn't just a cookbook; it's a passport to a world of flavors, a ticket to dinners that'll transport you across continents.

Now, you might be wondering, what's the deal with chicken? Well, it's more than just a protein. It's a canvas waiting for the stroke of culinary artistry, a chameleon that takes on flavors from every corner of the globe. This cookbook isn't just about recipes; it's about unleashing the potential of a versatile ingredient that has found its way into kitchens worldwide.

My inspiration for curating these global chicken recipes comes from the unifying power of food. Food isn't just sustenance; it's a cultural storyteller, a bridge between traditions and tastes. Whether it's the fiery spices of India, the aromatic herbs of the Mediterranean, or the smoky barbecue allure of the Americas - each recipe in this book carries a piece of the world's culinary tapestry.

What can you expect to find within these pages, you ask? Buckle up, because we're taking you on a tour that spans continents and flavors. From the comfort of your own kitchen, you'll be whipping up dishes that sing with the soul of Morocco's markets, the elegance of French bistros, and the vibrant chaos of Thai street food stalls.

Think succulent roasted chickens infused with fragrant spices, tender braised delights that melt in your mouth, and crispy-skinned wonders that'll have you reaching for seconds (and thirds). From the weeknight dinner rush to the gatherings that turn into unforgettable feasts, "Best of Chicken" has you covered.

So, get ready to roll up your sleeves, to wield your knives, to savor the sizzles and aromas that'll fill your kitchen. It's not just about cooking; it's about embarking on a culinary adventure that'll leave your palate richer and your dinner table more diverse. Welcome, my friends, to a world of chicken delights. The journey begins here, and I couldn't be more excited to have you on board.

# Cooking Philosophy or Approach

Now that we've laid the foundation, let's dive into the heart of the matter - my approach to cooking and the philosophy that underpins these tantalizing chicken recipes.

For me, cooking is more than just a chore; it's a sensory symphony, an act of storytelling that involves all five senses. It's about embracing the alchemy that happens when ingredients come together, about creating moments of connection around the dinner table. Cooking, at its core, is an expression of love and culture, and that's exactly what I've woven into the fabric of "Best of Chicken."

As you flip through these pages, you'll find that my approach is all about celebrating the diversity of flavors that this world has to offer. I've gathered recipes that span the globe, each with its own unique blend of spices, herbs, and techniques. From the simplicity of classic comfort food to the daring experimentation that pushes culinary boundaries - it's all here.

One thing you'll notice is my unwavering belief in the power of quality ingredients. Whether it's free-range organic chickens, locally sourced vegetables, or a medley of aromatic spices - the heart of a memorable dish lies in the raw materials. I encourage you to seek out the best you can find, and let those ingredients speak for themselves.

Techniques? Well, they're the secret sauce that transforms ingredients into masterpieces. From slow braising that coaxes out layers of flavor to quick searing that locks in juiciness, each technique is carefully chosen to showcase the potential of chicken in its myriad forms. And let's not forget the art of balancing flavors - the interplay of sweet and sour, salty and spicy - that creates a harmony that dances on your taste buds.

You'll find dishes that honor tradition, paying homage to the tried-and-true recipes that have stood the test of time. And alongside them, you'll discover innovative twists that bring modern flair to old favorites, a nod to the ever-evolving nature of gastronomy.

So, as you embark on this culinary journey, remember that cooking isn't just about following instructions; it's about channeling your creativity, adding a dash of your personality, and embracing the joy of experimentation. The kitchen is your playground, and "Best of Chicken" is your roadmap to culinary exploration. Get ready to wield your spatula with confidence, to infuse your dishes with passion, and to savor the delicious results of your culinary curiosity.

# Tips for Successful Cooking

Ahoy, fellow kitchen adventurers! Before you plunge into the aromatic world of chicken creations, let's arm you with some battle-tested wisdom that will ensure your culinary conquests are nothing short of triumphant.

**1. Choose Wisely:** When it comes to chicken, quality is king. Opt for free-range or organic poultry for a richer flavor and better texture. Trust me, your taste buds will thank you.

**2. Tempting Temps:** Cooking chicken is a delicate dance. Use a meat thermometer to ensure that the internal temperature reaches a safe 165°F (75°C). No room for guesswork here.

**3. Preheat Perfection:** Whether it's the oven or the skillet, preheating is your secret weapon. It ensures a sizzle, a sear, and that coveted golden crust.

**4. Brine Magic:** For juicy, succulent results, consider brining your chicken before cooking. A simple mix of water, salt, and maybe a touch of sugar can work wonders.

**5. Marinate with Gusto:** Marinating isn't just for show - it's a flavor-infusing ritual. Let your chicken soak in a concoction of herbs, spices, and acidic agents for a taste explosion.

**6. Patience Pays Off:** Rushing the cooking process is a surefire way to dry out your chicken. Low and slow is the name of the game, especially for tough cuts like thighs and legs.

**7. Cast Iron Charm:** A well-seasoned cast iron skillet is your go-to for achieving that crispy skin and that mouthwatering sear. Treat it right, and it'll be your trusty sidekick.

**8. Rest and Relax:** After the heat, comes the rest. Let your chicken sit for a few minutes before carving. This lets the juices redistribute, ensuring each bite is a succulent delight.

**9. Test the Waters:** Not all cuts are created equal. Lean breasts cook faster than robust thighs. Adjust your cooking times accordingly to avoid any undercooked surprises.

**10. Flavor Builders:** Don't underestimate the power of aromatics - garlic, onions, and herbs can elevate your dishes from good to exceptional.

**11. Dare to Dabble:** Don't shy away from experimentation. Add a splash of wine, a dash of spices, or a drizzle of honey - the kitchen is your playground, after all.

**12. Savvy Sides:** Pair your chicken with complementary sides that enhance the experience. Creamy mashed potatoes, vibrant salads, or perfectly roasted veggies - they all have their place at the table.

Remember, the kitchen is your canvas, and these tips are your brushstrokes. Embrace each step, celebrate the aromas that fill your home, and don't be afraid to make these recipes your own. As you stand before your stove, know that you're not just cooking - you're crafting memories, flavors, and experiences that will linger long after the meal is done. So, gather your tools, don your apron, and let's dive into the delicious world of chicken. Your culinary voyage starts now.

# Kitchen Essentials

Ahoy, kitchen maestros! As we embark on this chicken-themed culinary adventure, let's make sure you're well-equipped to conquer any culinary challenge that comes your way. Behold, your arsenal of kitchen essentials:

**1. Chef's Knife:** Your trusty companion for slicing, dicing, and chopping. Keep it sharp for smooth, precise cuts.

**2. Cutting Board:** A spacious cutting board gives you room to work your magic without making a mess.

**3. Cast Iron Skillet:** This heavyweight champion is your go-to for searing chicken to crispy perfection.

**4. Ovenproof Pan:** When you're finishing off your chicken in the oven, this pan is your ally.

**5. Meat Thermometer:** Don't play guessing games with doneness - let the meat thermometer be your guide.

**6. Tongs:** Your extended hands in the kitchen. Perfect for flipping, turning, and maneuvering chicken.

**7. Baking Sheet:** Whether it's for roasting or baking, a sturdy baking sheet is a must.

**8. Mixing Bowls:** Bowls of various sizes for mixing marinades, batters, and dressings.

**9. Whisk:** For combining liquids and emulsifying dressings with finesse.

**10. Garlic Press:** Save your fingers and infuse dishes with garlic goodness effortlessly.

**11. Zester/Grater:** Add a burst of citrus or finely grate cheese for that finishing touch.

**12. Blender/Food Processor:** These workhorses are essential for creating sauces, marinades, and more.

**13. Wooden Spoon:** Ideal for stirring sauces, soups, and stews without scratching your cookware.

**14. Kitchen Timer:** A reliable timer ensures your chicken is cooked to perfection.

**15. Measuring Cups and Spoons:** Precision matters – measure your ingredients accurately.

# Tips on How to Use These Tools Effectively

**Knife Skills:** Sharpen your knife skills to ensure safe and efficient slicing. The pinch grip is your friend.

**Preheating Prowess:** Preheat your skillet or pan before adding chicken for that satisfying sizzle.

**Thermometer Technique:** Insert the meat thermometer into the thickest part of the chicken, away from the bone, for accurate readings.

**Rest and Carve:** Let your chicken rest before carving to preserve those precious juices.

**Pan Prowess:** Master the art of searing by heating your skillet until it's smoking hot before adding chicken.

**Tongs Mastery:** Use tongs instead of forks to avoid piercing the chicken and letting the juices escape.

**Baking Brilliance:** Line your baking sheet with parchment paper to prevent sticking and make cleanup a breeze.

**Blender Magic:** When blending hot liquids, vent the lid slightly to release steam and prevent splatters.

**Grater Grace:** Use gentle pressure when zesting or grating to avoid including the bitter pith.

**Timely Triumph:** Set your kitchen timer to ensure your chicken is cooked to your desired doneness.

Armed with these tools and tips, you're ready to take on any chicken recipe with confidence. So, rally your kitchen companions, prepare to dazzle your taste buds, and let the flavors unfold in your culinary domain. Your kitchen is about to become the stage for a symphony of sizzles, aromas, and unforgettable tastes.

# Flavor Pairing Suggestions

Ahoy, flavor adventurers! As we navigate the seas of seasoning, it's time to unleash your inner culinary artist. Here are some flavor pairing inspirations that'll help you craft chicken masterpieces that sing with harmony and taste.

1. **Classic Mediterranean:** Embrace the allure of the Mediterranean with a marriage of olive oil, lemon, garlic, and rosemary. This timeless combination adds a touch of sunshine to your chicken.

2. **Spicy Fusion:** Elevate your chicken with a fiery dance of flavors. Pair it with a blend of cayenne, paprika, and cumin for a spicy sensation that'll awaken your taste buds.

3. **Asian Infusion:** Take a journey to the Far East with a fusion of soy sauce, ginger, and sesame. This trio brings a umami-rich depth to your dishes.

4. **Herb Garden Delight:** Experiment with a medley of fresh herbs like thyme, oregano, and basil. Their aromatic embrace transforms simple chicken into a fragrant symphony.

5. **Sweet and Savory:** Strike a balance between sweet and savory by drizzling honey or maple syrup over your chicken, then adding a sprinkle of crushed red pepper for a delightful contrast.

6. **Smoky Indulgence:** Embrace the smoky allure with a blend of smoked paprika, chipotle, and a hint of brown sugar. Your taste buds will embark on a flavor-filled journey.

7. **Tropical Tango:** Transport your senses to a tropical paradise by pairing chicken with a mix of coconut milk, lime, and a touch of ginger. It's a vacation on a plate.

8. **Tangy Elegance:** Liven up your chicken with a tangy twist. Combine balsamic vinegar, Dijon mustard, and a touch of honey for a sophisticated medley.

**9. Creamy Dream:** Indulge in the velvety charm of creamy sauces. A splash of heavy cream, Parmesan cheese, and a dash of nutmeg creates a luxurious texture.

**10. Nutty Delights:** Add a crunchy element with a handful of toasted nuts like almonds or walnuts. Their earthy richness complements the tender chicken.

**11. Garden Fresh:** Keep it light and refreshing with a blend of lemon zest, mint, and cucumber. It's a zesty and invigorating combination.

**12. Rustic Comfort:** Channel cozy vibes by pairing chicken with root vegetables like carrots, potatoes, and parsnips. The earthy flavors create a comforting embrace.

Remember, these pairings are just the beginning. Feel free to mix and match, to explore and experiment. Your kitchen is a canvas, and your palate is the brush. As you create your own culinary masterpieces, know that every combination is a stroke of your unique flavor artistry. So, embrace these suggestions, unleash your creativity, and let your chicken dishes tell stories as vibrant as your imagination. Bon appétit, my fellow flavor explorers!

# Index

# Chapter 1: Asian Inspirations

1 person | 600 calories | 45 minutes

# Hainanese Chicken Rice

Ah, the heavenly marriage of tender poached chicken and fragrant rice, a Singaporean classic that whispers tales of hawkers and heritage.
Prepare for an adventure in flavors!

## Ingredients:

- 1 whole chicken (about 3-4 lbs)
- 2 cups jasmine rice
- 4 cups chicken broth
- 4 slices ginger
- 3 cloves garlic
- 2 stalks lemongrass
- 2 tbsp vegetable oil
- Soy sauce and sesame oil for serving

## Directions

1. Rub chicken with salt and rinse.
2. Cook rice in chicken broth.
3. Sauté ginger, garlic, and lemongrass.
4. Poach chicken in aromatic broth.
5. Slice and serve with rice, soy sauce, and sesame oil.

## Substitutions

- Ginger for lemongrass
- Chicken thighs for a leaner option
- Brown rice
- Homemade chicken broth
- Chilli sauce with ginger and garlic
- Cucumber slices

1
person

450
calories

60
minutes

# Tandoori Chicken

In the heart of India, smoky tandoori ovens birthed this masterpiece. Marinated in yogurt and spices, it's a symphony of flavors. Get ready for a mouthful of culture.

## Ingredients:

- 2 lbs chicken pieces
- 1 cup plain yogurt
- 2 tbsp tandoori masala
- 1 tbsp ginger-garlic paste
- 1 tsp turmeric
- 1 tsp cayenne pepper
- Salt to taste

## Directions

1. Score chicken and mix marinade ingredients.
2. Coat chicken in marinade and refrigerate for a few hours.
3. Preheat grill or oven.
4. Grill or bake until charred and cooked.
5. Serve with naan.

## Substitutions

- Kashmiri red chili powder for milder heat
- Ghee for richness
- Lemon juice for tang
- Chaat masala for a zesty twist
- Greek yogurt instead of regular yogurt

1
person

500
calories

50
minutes

# Korean Fried Chicken

Crispy, golden, and coated in a finger-licking sauce, Korean fried chicken dances between sweet and spicy.
Soul food that ignites your senses!

## Ingredients:

- 2 lbs chicken wings
- 1 cup potato starch
- Oil for frying
- 1/2 cup gochujang
- 1/4 cup soy sauce
- 2 tbsp rice vinegar
- 1/4 cup honey
- 2 cloves garlic
- Sesame seeds and chopped scallions for garnish

## Directions

1. Toss wings in potato starch and fry twice.
2. Combine gochujang, soy sauce, vinegar, honey, and garlic.
3. Cook sauce until thick.
4. Coat wings in sauce.
5. Garnish and serve with pickled radishes.

## Substitutions

- Cornstarch instead of potato starch
- Sriracha for heat
- Brown sugar for honey
- Apple cider vinegar for rice vinegar
- Toasted sesame oil for nutty flavor
- Cilantro for scallions

1
person

550
calories

40
minutes

# Pad Thai with Chicken

From the bustling streets of Thailand, this stir-fried noodle sensation is sweet, savory, and utterly addictive.
A whirlwind of tastes that'll transport you to Bangkok.

## Ingredients:

- 6 oz rice noodles
- 2 chicken breasts
- 3 cloves garlic
- 2 eggs
- 1 cup bean sprouts
- 1/4 cup crushed peanuts
- 2 tbsp vegetable oil
- 3 tbsp tamarind paste
- 2 tbsp fish sauce

## Directions

1. Soak noodles and slice chicken.
2. Sauté garlic and add chicken.
3. Push chicken to the side, scramble eggs.
4. Add noodles, tamarind, and fish sauce.
5. Toss and add bean sprouts and peanuts.

## Substitutions

- Shrimp instead of chicken
- Lime juice for tang
- Palm sugar for sweetness
- Sriracha for heat
- Cilantro and lime wedges for garnish

1
person

400
calories

35
minutes

# Teriyaki Chicken

The graceful simplicity of Japanese cuisine shines through teriyaki. Succulent chicken glazed in a soy-based elixir.
A brushstroke of umami in every bite.

## Ingredients:

- 2 chicken thighs
- 1/4 cup soy sauce
- 2 tbsp sake
- 2 tbsp mirin
- 1 tbsp sugar
- 1 clove garlic
- 1 tsp ginger
- 1 tbsp vegetable oil

## Directions

1. Mix soy sauce, sake, mirin, sugar, garlic, and ginger for marinade.
2. Marinate chicken for 20 min.
3. Sear chicken and reduce marinade.
4. Glaze chicken with reduced sauce.
5. Serve with steamed rice.

## Substitutions

- Chicken breasts for a leaner option
- Honey for sweetness
- Rice wine vinegar for mirin
- Sesame seeds for garnish
- Steamed broccoli on the side

1 person

700 calories

75 minutes

# Biryani with Chicken

Pakistan's prized gem, biryani, whispers stories of regality and love. Fragrant rice layered with spiced chicken.
Each bite a tapestry of history and flavor.

## Ingredients:

- 1 cup basmati rice
- 1 chicken leg quarter
- 1/2 cup yogurt
- 1 onion
- 2 cloves garlic
- 1/2 inch ginger
- 1/4 tsp each of cumin, coriander, garam masala
- Saffron strands
- Ghee

## Directions

1. Marinate chicken in yogurt and spices.
2. Sauté onions, garlic, and ginger.
3. Parboil rice and layer with chicken.
4. Add saffron and ghee.
5. Cover and cook until rice is fluffy.
6. Uncover, and savor.

## Substitutions

- Lamb or beef instead of chicken
- Birista (fried onions) for garnish
- Rose water for saffron
- Cashews and raisins for richness
- Mint and cilantro chutney for a refreshing kick

1 person

480 calories

55 minutes

# Lemongrass Chicken

Vietnam's lemongrass chicken dances between citrusy brightness and savory depth. Each bite a tantalizing journey through the streets of Hanoi.
A flavor expedition.

## Ingredients:

- 2 chicken thighs
- 2 stalks lemongrass
- 3 cloves garlic
- 1 shallot
- 1 chili
- 2 tbsp fish sauce
- 1 tbsp soy sauce
- 1 tbsp sugar
- Oil for cooking
- Fresh herbs for garnish

## Directions

1. Blend lemongrass, garlic, shallot, and chili.
2. Sauté lemongrass mixture.
3. Add chicken, fish sauce, soy sauce, and sugar.
4. Sear until caramelized.
5. Garnish and serve with steamed rice.

## Substitutions

- Lemongrass paste for fresh lemongrass
- Sriracha for heat
- Palm sugar for authenticity
- Jasmine rice
- Lime wedges for tang
- Crushed peanuts for crunch

1
person

520
calories

40
minutes

# Cashew Chicken

China's culinary wizardry shines in cashew chicken. Succulent bites of chicken, crunchy cashews, and vibrant vegetables unite. A wok-tossed symphony of textures.

## Ingredients:

- 1 chicken breast
- 1/2 cup roasted cashews
- 1 red bell pepper
- 1/2 onion
- 2 cloves garlic
- 2 tbsp soy sauce
- 1 tbsp oyster sauce
- 1 tsp hoisin sauce
- 1 tsp cornstarch
- Green onions for garnish

## Directions

1. Sauté chicken until cooked and set aside.
2. Sauté garlic, onion, and bell pepper.
3. Mix sauces and cornstarch.
4. Toss chicken and cashews in sauce.
5. Garnish and serve over steamed rice.

## Substitutions

- Broccoli florets for crunch
- Dark soy sauce for color
- Shrimp or tofu instead of chicken
- Rice vinegar for tang
- Sesame seeds for garnish
- Bok choy for a veggie twist

1 person
580 calories
50 minutes

# Chicken Adobo

The Philippines' embrace of vinegar and soy births chicken adobo. A harmonious blend of sweet, salty, and tangy.
Each bite a salute to island life.

## Ingredients:

- 2 chicken thighs
- 1/3 cup vinegar
- 1/4 cup soy sauce
- 3 cloves garlic
- 1 bay leaf
- 1 tsp peppercorns
- 1 tsp brown sugar
- Oil for cooking
- Hard-boiled eggs for serving

## Directions

1. Marinate chicken in vinegar, soy sauce, garlic, bay leaf, and peppercorns.
2. Sear chicken and set aside.
3. Make a sauce with the marinade and sugar.
4. Simmer chicken in sauce.
5. Serve with rice and eggs.

## Substitutions

- Coconut aminos for soy sauce
- Palm vinegar for authenticity
- Coconut sugar for brown sugar
- Chili peppers for heat
- Steamed bok choy for freshness
- Pickled papaya on the side

1 person | 650 calories | 65 minutes

# Malaysian Curry Chicken

Malaysia's curry chicken unveils a tapestry of spices. Tender meat and potatoes bathe in a rich coconut curry.
A feast that echoes the diversity of Malaysia.

## Ingredients:

- 1 chicken leg quarter
- 1 potato
- 1/2 cup coconut milk
- 1/2 cup chicken broth
- 2 tbsp Malaysian curry powder
- 1 onion
- 2 cloves garlic
- 1 lemongrass
- Oil for cooking
- Fresh cilantro for garnish

## Directions

1. Sauté onion, garlic, and lemongrass.
2. Add curry powder and cook until fragrant.
3. Add chicken and sear.
4. Add coconut milk and broth.
5. Simmer until chicken is cooked and potatoes are tender.
6. Garnish and devour.

## Substitutions

- Chicken breasts for a leaner option
- Sweet potatoes for a twist
- Kaffir lime leaves for lemongrass
- Thai basil for cilantro
- Roti canai for dipping
- Cucumber salad on the side

# Chapter 2: Flavors of the Americas

1 person | 600 calories | 45 minutes

# Southern Fried Chicken

Ah, the South's secret weapon: crispy, golden fried chicken. A melody of crunch and succulence that echoes through time.

## Ingredients:

- 2 chicken leg quarters
- 1 cup buttermilk
- 2 cups flour
- 2 tbsp paprika
- 1 tbsp garlic powder
- Oil for frying
- Salt and pepper

## Directions

1. Soak chicken in buttermilk.
2. Mix flour and spices.
3. Dredge chicken in flour mixture.
4. Fry until golden and cooked.
5. Drain on paper towels.
6. Season with salt and pepper.
7. Dive in!

## Substitutions

- Hot sauce in the buttermilk for heat
- Cornmeal for a crunchier coating
- Cajun seasoning for a kick
- Serve with collard greens and cornbread
- Pickles on the side
- Drizzle honey for sweetness

1
person

450
calories

55
minutes

# Chicken Enchiladas

Mexico's gift, enchiladas, are a symphony of tender chicken wrapped in corn tortillas and smothered in rich sauce.

## Ingredients:

- 2 chicken breasts
- 8 corn tortillas
- 1 cup red enchilada sauce
- 1 cup shredded cheese
- 1/2 cup chopped onion
- 1/4 cup chopped cilantro
- Sour cream and lime wedges for serving

## Directions

1. Cook and shred chicken.
2. Warm tortillas and dip in sauce.
3. Fill with chicken and roll.
4. Place in baking dish.
5. Top with sauce and cheese.
6. Bake until bubbly.
7. Garnish and serve.

## Substitutions

- Ground beef or beans instead of chicken
- Green enchilada sauce for a tangy twist
- Jalapeños for heat
- Avocado slices for richness
- Serve with rice and black beans
- Pickled red onions on top

1 person | 500 calories | 60 minutes

# Peruvian Roast Chicken

Peru's secret weapon, pollo a la brasa, is a masterpiece of flavors. A juicy, spiced roast chicken that reigns supreme.

## Ingredients:

- 1 whole chicken
- 2 tbsp soy sauce
- 2 tbsp vinegar
- 1 tbsp paprika
- 1 tsp cumin
- 1 tsp oregano
- 3 cloves garlic
- Oil for cooking
- Salt and pepper
- Aji sauce for dipping

## Directions

1. Blend marinade ingredients.
2. Rub chicken with marinade.
3. Roast until golden and cooked.
4. Slice and serve with aji sauce.
5. Savor the flavors of the Andes.

## Substitutions

- Pisco for authenticity
- Smoked paprika for depth
- Roast potatoes on the side
- Serve with quinoa salad
- Drizzle olive oil for richness
- Chicha morada for a traditional Peruvian drink

1 person | 620 calories | 120 minutes

# Brazilian Chicken Feijoada

Brazil's feijoada is a carnival of flavors, a stew of black beans, chicken, and sausage. A feast that celebrates life.

## Ingredients:

- 1 chicken leg quarter
- 1/2 cup black beans
- 1/4 cup chopped chorizo
- 1/4 cup chopped bacon
- 1/2 onion
- 2 cloves garlic
- 1 bay leaf
- Rice and orange slices for serving

## Directions

1. Sauté onion, garlic, chorizo, and bacon.
2. Add chicken and sear.
3. Add beans, bay leaf, and water.
4. Simmer until beans are tender.
5. Serve with rice and orange slices.
6. Savor the samba.

## Substitutions

- Pork sausage instead of chorizo
- Collard greens for a traditional side
- Farofa (toasted cassava flour) for crunch
- Passion fruit caipirinha for a refreshing sip
- Play samba music in the background

1 person

480 calories

50 minutes

# Jamaican Jerk Chicken

Jamaica's jerk chicken is a fiery dance of flavors. Marinated in a blend of spices, it's a taste of the Caribbean sun.

## Ingredients:

- 2 chicken thighs
- 2 tbsp jerk seasoning
- 2 tbsp soy sauce
- 2 tbsp brown sugar
- 1 lime
- 1 scotch bonnet pepper
- 2 cloves garlic
- Oil for cooking
- Fresh thyme for garnish

## Directions

1. Blend jerk seasoning, soy sauce, sugar, lime, pepper, and garlic.
2. Marinate chicken in mixture.
3. Sear chicken until charred.
4. Finish cooking in the oven.
5. Garnish and limbo into flavor.

## Substitutions

- Habanero pepper for scotch bonnet
- Allspice berries for a traditional touch
- Coconut rice and peas on the side
- Mango salsa for a tropical twist
- Serve with Jamaican ginger beer

1 person | 550 calories | 45 minutes

# Argentinian Chimichurri Chicken

Argentina's chimichurri chicken is a tango of flavors. Grilled chicken doused in vibrant herb sauce that dances on your palate.

## Ingredients:

- 2 chicken breasts
- 1/2 cup fresh parsley
- 1/4 cup fresh cilantro
- 2 cloves garlic
- 1/4 cup red wine vinegar
- 1/2 cup olive oil
- Red pepper flakes to taste
- Salt and pepper

## Directions

1. Blend herbs, garlic, vinegar, and oil.
2. Marinate chicken in half the sauce.
3. Grill chicken until cooked.
4. Drizzle with remaining sauce.
5. Tango with the tangy flavors.

## Substitutions

- Oregano for a traditional touch
- Lemon juice for a citrusy kick
- Grilled vegetables on the side
- Serve with Argentine Malbec wine
- Chimichurri dipping sauce for bread
- Crispy potatoes underneath

1 person

680 calories

40 minutes

# Chicken and Waffles

A Southern love affair, chicken and waffles unite sweet and savory. Crispy fried chicken atop fluffy waffles.A duet that soothes the soul.

## Ingredients:

- 1 chicken leg quarter
- 1 cup waffle batter
- Oil for frying
- Butter and maple syrup for serving
- Fresh parsley for garnish

## Directions

1. Fry chicken until golden and cooked.
2. Make waffle batter and cook until golden.
3. Top waffles with chicken.
4. Drizzle with syrup and butter.
5. Garnish and hum along with happiness.

## Substitutions

- Chicken tenders for smaller bites
- Bacon-infused waffle batter for extra flair
- Hot sauce for a spicy twist
- Serve with buttermilk gravy
- Fresh berries for a burst of color
- Blueberry syrup

1 person | 520 calories | 50 minutes

# Cuban Arroz con Pollo

Cuba's arroz con pollo is a melody of flavors. Tender chicken and saffron-infused rice dance in harmony.
A taste of Havana.

## Ingredients:

- 1 chicken thigh
- 1/2 cup rice
- 1/2 onion
- 1/2 bell pepper
- 1/4 cup frozen peas
- 2 cloves garlic
- 1/4 tsp saffron threads
- 1/2 cup chicken broth
- 1 tbsp olive oil

## Directions

1. Sauté onion, pepper, and garlic.
2. Add rice and saffron.
3. Sear chicken and add to the pot.
4. Add broth and peas.
5. Simmer until rice is tender.
6. Experience Havana's essence.

## Substitutions

- Annatto seeds for saffron
- Tomato sauce for a touch of sweetness
- Black beans on the side
- Serve with Cuban coffee
- Fried plantains for a taste of the tropics
- Lime wedge for tang

1
person

580
calories

60
minutes

# Chicken Mole

Mexico's mole is a complex symphony of flavors. Tender chicken immersed in a rich sauce made from chiles and chocolate.

## Ingredients:

- 1 chicken breast
- 2 dried ancho chiles
- 1 dried mulato chile
- 1/4 cup almonds
- 1/4 cup raisins
- 2 tbsp sesame seeds
- 1 clove garlic
- 1/4 tsp cinnamon
- 1 oz dark chocolate

## Directions

1. Toast chiles, almonds, raisins, and seeds.
2. Blend with garlic, cinnamon, and chocolate.
3. Sear chicken and add sauce.
4. Simmer until chicken is cooked.
5. Dive into the depth of flavors.

## Substitutions

- Poblano pepper for ancho chiles
- Honey for sweetness
- Ground cloves for warmth
- Serve with Mexican rice and refried beans
- Fresh cilantro and queso fresco for garnish
- Sip on horchata

1 person | 650 calories | 40 minutes

# Canadian Poutine with Chicken

Canada's poutine with chicken is a warm embrace of comfort. Crispy fries and cheese curds, topped with tender chicken.

## Ingredients:

- 1 chicken breast
- 1 cup frozen French fries
- 1/2 cup cheese curds
- 1/4 cup chicken gravy
- 2 tbsp chopped green onions

## Directions

1. Cook chicken until golden and cooked.
2. Cook fries until crispy.
3. Assemble fries, curds, and chicken.
4. Drizzle with gravy.
5. Garnish with green onions.
6. Feel the Canadian coziness.

## Substitutions

- Gravy made with turkey stock for authenticity
- Sweet potato fries for a twist
- Curly cheese curds for extra gooeyness
- Serve with Canadian craft beer
- Caramelized onions for added flavor

# Chapter 3: European Delights

1
person

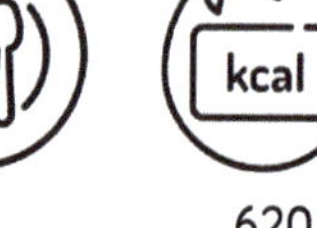
620
calories

120
minutes

# Coq au Vin

France's coq au vin is a symphony of sophistication. Tender chicken, red wine, and mushrooms come together in perfect harmony.

## Ingredients:

- 1 chicken leg quarter
- 1/2 cup red wine
- 1/2 cup chicken broth
- 2 slices bacon
- 1/2 onion
- 2 cloves garlic
- 1 carrot
- 8 oz mushrooms
- Fresh thyme and parsley for garnish

## Directions

1. Sauté bacon, onion, and garlic.
2. Add chicken and sear.
3. Add wine and broth.
4. Simmer until chicken is cooked.
5. Sauté mushrooms and add to the pot.
6. Garnish with herbs.
7. Indulge.

## Substitutions

- Red wine for authenticity
- Pearl onions for sweetness
- Serve with crusty baguette
- Ratatouille on the side
- Brie cheese for a French touch
- Escargot for adventurous eaters

1
person

580
calories

50
minutes

# Chicken Kiev

Ukraine's chicken kiev is a burst of flavors. Succulent chicken wrapped around herbed butter, a surprise waiting to be unveiled.

## Ingredients:

- 1 chicken breast
- 2 tbsp butter
- 1 clove garlic
- 1 tbsp chopped parsley
- 1/4 cup flour
- 1 egg
- 1/2 cup breadcrumbs
- Oil for frying

## Directions

1. Mix butter, garlic, and parsley.
2. Flatten chicken and wrap around butter mixture.
3. Coat in flour, dip in egg, and coat in breadcrumbs.
4. Fry until golden.
5. Slice and let the butter ooze out.

## Substitutions

- Herbed cream cheese for butter
- Chopped dill for a Ukrainian touch
- Serve with borscht soup
- Smetana (sour cream) for dipping
- Pickled vegetables on the side
- Vodka shots for a true Ukrainian experience

1
person

620
calories

60
minutes

# Spanish Chicken Paella

Spain's paella is a canvas of flavors. Saffron-infused rice, tender chicken, and an array of seafood. A taste of the Mediterranean.

## Ingredients:

- 1 chicken thigh
- 1/2 cup paella rice
- 1/4 cup diced tomatoes
- 1/4 cup chopped bell pepper
- 1/4 cup peas
- 1/4 cup shrimp
- 1/4 cup mussels
- 1/4 cup squid rings
- Saffron threads

## Directions

1. Sear chicken until golden.
2. Sauté rice, tomatoes, and peppers.
3. Add saffron and broth.
4. Nestle chicken and seafood into the rice.
5. Simmer until rice is tender.
6. Dive into the flavors of Spain.

## Substitutions

- Chorizo for a smoky kick
- Clams for mussels
- Artichoke hearts for a twist
- Serve with sangria
- Churros with chocolate dip for dessert
- Enjoy while watching flamenco dancers

1 person

550 calories

40 minutes

# Greek Souvlaki

Greece's souvlaki is a breeze of flavors. Marinated chicken skewers grilled to perfection, a taste of the Mediterranean sun.

## Ingredients:

- 2 chicken breasts
- 1/4 cup Greek yogurt
- 2 tbsp lemon juice
- 1 tsp dried oregano
- 1/4 tsp garlic powder
- Pita bread
- Diced cucumber, tomato, and red onion for serving

## Directions

1. Mix yogurt, lemon juice, oregano, and garlic powder.
2. Marinate chicken in mixture.
3. Skewer chicken and grill until cooked.
4. Serve in pita with fresh veggies.
5. Transport yourself to the Greek isles.

## Substitutions

- Lamb or pork instead of chicken
- Tzatziki sauce for dipping
- Kalamata olives and feta cheese for authenticity
- Greek salad on the side
- Ouzo shots for a festive touch
- Zorba's dance in the background

1
person

620
calories

50
minutes

# Italian Chicken Parmesan

Italy's chicken parmesan is a comfort classic. Breaded chicken, melted cheese, and tomato sauce create a culinary hug.

## Ingredients:

- 1 chicken breast
- 1/4 cup breadcrumbs
- 1/4 cup grated parmesan
- 1/2 cup marinara sauce
- 1/4 cup shredded mozzarella
- Fresh basil leaves for garnish

## Directions

1. Mix breadcrumbs and parmesan.
2. Coat chicken in mixture.
3. Fry until golden.
4. Top with marinara and mozzarella.
5. Bake until cheese melts.
6. Garnish with basil.
7. Melt into Italian flavors.

## Substitutions

- Italian seasoning for extra flavor
- Spaghetti on the side
- Serve with a Chianti wine
- Tiramisu for dessert
- Italian opera music playing softly
- Speak with your hands while enjoying

1
person

580
calories

45
minutes

# Swiss Chicken Cordon Bleu

Switzerland's cordon bleu is a symphony of textures. Breaded chicken stuffed with ham and melted cheese, a Swiss delight.

## Ingredients:

- 1 chicken breast
- 2 slices ham
- 2 slices Swiss cheese
- 1/4 cup flour
- 1 egg
- 1/2 cup breadcrumbs
- Oil for frying

## Directions

1. Flatten chicken and layer ham and cheese.
2. Fold and secure with toothpicks.
3. Coat in flour, dip in egg, and coat in breadcrumbs.
4. Fry until golden.
5. Melt into the gooey goodness.

## Substitutions

- Gruyère cheese for Swiss cheese
- Prosciutto for ham
- Rösti potatoes on the side
- Serve with Swiss chocolate fondue
- Enjoy while watching the Alps
- Yodel softly in the background

1 person | 540 calories | 55 minutes

# Portuguese Chicken Piri Piri

Portugal's piri piri chicken is a blaze of flavors. Marinated in fiery chili sauce, it's a journey to the sunny shores of Portugal.

## Ingredients:

- 1 chicken thigh
- 2 tbsp piri piri sauce
- 1 lemon
- 2 cloves garlic
- 1/4 tsp paprika
- 1/4 tsp cumin
- Olive oil for cooking

## Directions

1. Mix piri piri sauce, lemon juice, garlic, paprika, and cumin.
2. Marinate chicken in mixture.
3. Sear chicken until cooked.
4. Drizzle with olive oil.
5. Experience the thrill of Portugal.

## Substitutions

- Bird's eye chili for authentic piri piri
- Serve with Portuguese vinho verde wine
- Bacalhau (salted cod) on the side
- Pasteis de nata for dessert
- Fado music playing softly in the background

1
person

620
calories

60
minutes

# British Chicken Tikka Masala

Britain's tikka masala is a taste of culinary fusion. Tender chicken in creamy tomato sauce, a comforting embrace of flavors.

## Ingredients:

- 1 chicken breast
- 1/4 cup plain yogurt
- 1/4 cup tomato sauce
- 1/4 cup heavy cream
- 1 tsp garam masala
- 1/4 tsp turmeric
- 1/4 tsp cumin
- 1/4 tsp paprika
- Fresh cilantro for garnish

## Directions

1. Mix yogurt, tomato sauce, cream, and spices.
2. Marinate chicken in mixture.
3. Sear chicken until cooked.
4. Simmer in remaining sauce.
5. Garnish with cilantro.
6. Savor the British-Indian fusion.

## Substitutions

- Serve with naan bread
- Mango chutney for sweetness
- Onion bhaji on the side
- Drink with a pint of British ale
- Listen to The Beatles while enjoying
- Use a British accent for an authentic experience

1
person

540
calories

55
minutes

# Hungarian Chicken Paprikash

Hungary's chicken paprikash is a warm hug of flavors. Tender chicken in creamy paprika sauce, a taste of Hungarian comfort.

## Ingredients:

- 1 chicken thigh
- 1/2 onion
- 2 cloves garlic
- 1 tbsp sweet paprika
- 1/4 cup sour cream
- Fresh parsley for garnish

## Directions

1. Sauté onion and garlic.
2. Add paprika and sear chicken.
3. Add water and simmer.
4. Stir in sour cream.
5. Garnish with parsley.
6. Revel in the comfort of Hungary.

## Substitutions

- Serve with Hungarian dumplings (nokedli)
- Sip on pálinka (fruit brandy)
- Hungarian goulash on the side
- Listen to traditional Hungarian folk music
- Wear a Hungarian embroidered shirt

1 person | 570 calories | 50 minutes

# Swedish Chicken Meatballs

Sweden's chicken meatballs are a playful delight. Tender chicken, seasoned to perfection, and smothered in creamy gravy.

## Ingredients:

- 1 chicken breast
- 1/4 cup breadcrumbs
- 1/4 cup milk
- 1/4 tsp nutmeg
- 1/4 tsp allspice
- 1/4 tsp onion powder
- 1/4 tsp garlic powder
- Lingonberry sauce for serving

## Directions

1. Mix breadcrumbs and milk.
2. Combine with chicken and spices.
3. Shape into meatballs and sear.
4. Make creamy gravy.
5. Serve meatballs with gravy and lingonberry sauce.
6. Embrace Swedish whimsy.

## Substitutions

- Serve with creamy mashed potatoes
- Dill for garnish
- Drink lingonberry juice
- Listen to ABBA's greatest hits while enjoying
- Dance like a Swede around the kitchen

# Chapter 4: Taste of the Middle East

1 person | 560 calories | 60 minutes

# Shawarma Chicken

## Ingredients:

- 1 chicken thigh
- 1/4 cup plain yogurt
- 2 tbsp olive oil
- 1 tsp cumin
- 1 tsp paprika
- 1/2 tsp turmeric
- Pita bread
- Sliced cucumber, tomato, and onion for serving

The Middle East's shawarma is a flavor explosion. Marinated chicken slices, slow-cooked to perfection, a journey to culinary bliss.

## Directions

1. Mix yogurt, oil, and spices.
2. Marinate chicken in mixture.
3. Thread chicken onto skewers and slow-cook.
4. Serve in pita with veggies.
5. Immerse yourself in the flavors of the Middle East.

## Substitutions

- Sumac for a tangy kick
- Tahini sauce for dipping
- Fries inside the pita for a twist
- Serve with mint tea
- Listen to Arabic music while enjoying
- Attempt belly dancing after the meal

1 person | 610 calories | 80 minutes

Morocco's chicken tagine is a fragrant journey. Tender chicken, dried fruits, and warm spices dance in a clay pot.

# Moroccan Chicken Tagine

## Ingredients:

- 1 chicken leg quarter
- 1/4 cup dried apricots
- 1/4 cup almonds
- 1/2 onion
- 2 cloves garlic
- 1/2 tsp cumin
- 1/2 tsp cinnamon
- 1/4 tsp ginger
- Fresh cilantro for garnish

## Directions

1. Sauté onion and garlic.
2. Add spices and sear chicken.
3. Add dried fruits and almonds.
4. Simmer in water.
5. Garnish with cilantro.
6. Savor the flavors of Morocco.

## Substitutions

- Preserved lemons for authenticity
- Serve with couscous
- Moroccan mint tea on the side
- Listen to Moroccan folk music
- Sit on a colorful rug while enjoying
- Wear a fez hat for extra flair

1
person

590
calories

70
minutes

# Persian Saffron Chicken

Iran's saffron chicken is a golden delight. Marinated in saffron and yogurt, it's a taste of Persian opulence.

## Ingredients:

- 1 chicken breast
- 1/4 cup plain yogurt
- 1/4 tsp saffron threads
- 1/4 tsp turmeric
- 1/4 tsp cardamom
- Basmati rice
- Barberries and slivered pistachios for garnish

## Directions

1. Mix yogurt, saffron, turmeric, and cardamom.
2. Marinate chicken in mixture.
3. Grill until golden.
4. Serve over rice.
5. Garnish with barberries and pistachios.
6. Bask in Persian luxury.

## Substitutions

- Serve with Iranian saffron rice (zereshk polo)
- Iranian tea with rock sugar for sweetness
- Listen to Persian classical music
- Enjoy on a Persian carpet
- Wear a Persian-style shawl

1
person

530
calories

50
minutes

# Israeli Chicken Schnitzel

Israel's schnitzel is a crispy delight. Breaded chicken cutlet fried to perfection, a taste of Israeli street food.

## Ingredients:

- 1 chicken breast
- 1/4 cup flour
- 1 egg
- 1/2 cup breadcrumbs
- Oil for frying
- Hummus and pita bread for serving

## Directions

1. Flatten chicken and coat in flour.
2. Dip in egg and coat in breadcrumbs.
3. Fry until golden.
4. Serve with hummus and pita.
5. Crunch into the flavors of Israel.

## Substitutions

- Za'atar seasoning for extra flavor
- Israeli salad on the side
- Enjoy with a glass of Israeli wine
- Listen to Hebrew pop music
- Imagine strolling through the streets of Tel Aviv while enjoying

1
person

560
calories

60
minutes

# Lebanese Chicken Kebabs

Lebanon's chicken kebabs are a culinary dance. Marinated chicken skewers grilled to perfection, a taste of Lebanese charm.

## Ingredients:

- 2 chicken thighs
- 1/4 cup plain yogurt
- 2 tbsp lemon juice
- 1/2 onion
- 2 cloves garlic
- 1/4 tsp cumin
- 1/4 tsp paprika
- Flatbread
- Chopped parsley and sumac for garnish

## Directions

1. Mix yogurt, lemon juice, onion, garlic, cumin, and paprika.
2. Marinate chicken in mixture.
3. Skewer and grill until cooked.
4. Serve in flatbread with herbs and sumac.
5. Dance with Lebanese flavors.

## Substitutions

- Serve with tahini sauce
- Pickled turnips on the side
- Arabic coffee for a traditional touch
- Listen to Lebanese oud music
- Dance the dabke while enjoying

1
person

590
calories

70
minutes

# Egyptian Chicken Molokhia

Egypt's molokhia is a hearty embrace. Chicken simmered in a green leafy stew, a taste of Egyptian comfort.

## Ingredients:

- 1 chicken leg quarter
- 1/2 cup dried molokhia leaves
- 1/4 cup chopped onion
- 2 cloves garlic
- 1/4 tsp ground coriander
- 1/4 tsp ground cumin
- Basmati rice for serving

## Directions

1. Sauté onion and garlic.
2. Add chicken and sear.
3. Add molokhia and spices.
4. Simmer until chicken is cooked.
5. Serve over rice.
6. Relish the flavors of Egypt.

## Substitutions

- Fresh molokhia leaves for authenticity
- Serve with Egyptian baladi bread
- Hibiscus tea on the side
- Listen to Egyptian oud music
- Imagine cruising down the Nile while enjoying

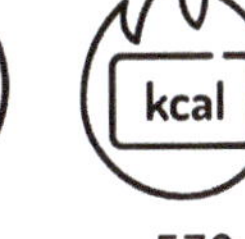

1 person | 570 calories | 60 minutes

# Turkish Chicken Kebabs

Turkey's chicken kebabs are a taste of tradition. Marinated chicken skewers grilled to perfection, a culinary journey to Turkey.

## Ingredients:

- 2 chicken breasts
- 1/4 cup plain yogurt
- 2 tbsp olive oil
- 1 tbsp tomato paste
- 1 tsp paprika
- 1/2 tsp cumin
- Flatbread
- Sliced red onion and parsley for garnish

## Directions

1. Mix yogurt, oil, tomato paste, paprika, and cumin.
2. Marinate chicken in mixture.
3. Skewer and grill until cooked.
4. Serve in flatbread with onion and parsley.
5. Embark on a Turkish delight.

## Substitutions

- Pomegranate molasses for a tangy kick
- Serve with Turkish tea
- Baklava for dessert
- Listen to Turkish classical music
- Imagine exploring the bazaars of Istanbul while enjoying

1
person

610
calories

90
minutes

# Jordanian Mansaf

Jordan's mansaf is a royal feast. Tender chicken atop fragrant rice, drizzled with tangy yogurt sauce, a taste of Jordanian hospitality.

## Ingredients:

- 1 chicken thigh
- 1/2 cup long-grain rice
- 1/4 cup chopped onion
-1/4 cupdried jameed (fermented yogurt)
- 2 cloves garlic
- Almonds and fresh parsley for garnish

## Directions

1. Sauté onion and garlic.
2. Add rice and water.
3. Sear chicken and add to the pot.
4. Simmer with jameed.
5. Serve over rice and garnish with almonds and parsley.
6. Experience Jordan's warmth.

## Substitutions

- Pine nuts for a crunch
- Serve with Jordanian tea
- Traditional Bedouin music in the background
- Enjoy while surrounded by desert scenery
- Wear a kufiya (traditional headdress) for added authenticity

1 person

590 calories

80 minutes

# Iraqi Chicken Quzi

Iraq's chicken quzi is a symphony of flavors. Slow-cooked chicken, fragrant rice, and toasted nuts, a taste of Iraqi celebration.

## Ingredients:

- 1 chicken leg quarter
- 1/2 cup basmati rice
- 1/4 cup chopped onion
- 2 cloves garlic
- 1/4 tsp ground cinnamon
- 1/4 tsp ground cardamom
- Almonds and raisins for garnish

## Directions

1. Sauté onion and garlic.
2. Add rice and spices.
3. Sear chicken and add to the pot.
4. Slow-cook until rice is tender.
5. Serve over rice and garnish with almonds and raisins.
6. Revel in Iraqi flavors.

## Substitutions

- Serve with Iraqi flatbread
- Enjoy with black tea and cardamom
- Listen to traditional Iraqi maqam music
- Picture yourself in the ancient city of Babylon while enjoying

1 person | 600 calories | 70 minutes

# Yemeni Saltah with Chicken

Yemen's saltah is a bowl of comfort. Slow-cooked chicken stew, topped with a dollop of fenugreek-infused yogurt, a taste of Yemeni coziness.

## Ingredients:

- 1 chicken thigh
- 1/4 cup chopped onion
- 2 cloves garlic
- 1/4 tsp ground cumin
- 1/4 tsp ground coriander
- Fenugreek-infused yogurt for serving

## Directions

1. Sauté onion and garlic.
2. Add chicken and sear.
3. Add spices and water.
4. Simmer until chicken is cooked.
5. Serve in a bowl with fenugreek yogurt.
6. Experience the warmth of Yemen.

## Substitutions

- Serve with Yemeni flatbread (malawach)
- Sip on qishr (Yemeni spiced coffee)
- Listen to traditional Yemeni music
- Imagine the bustling markets of Sana'a while enjoying

# Chapter 5: African Flavors

1
person

580
calories

70
minutes

# Senegalese Chicken Yassa

Senegal's yassa is a burst of flavors. Marinated chicken simmered with caramelized onions and tangy mustard, a taste of West Africa.

## Ingredients:

- 1 chicken leg quarter
- 1/4 cup chopped onion
- 2 cloves garlic
- 1/4 cup lemon juice
- 1/4 cup Dijon mustard
- Fresh parsley for garnish

## Directions

1. Sauté onion and garlic.
2. Marinate chicken in lemon juice and mustard.
3. Sear chicken and add to the pot.
4. Simmer until chicken is cooked.
5. Serve with caramelized onions.
6. Delight in Senegalese flair.

## Substitutions

- Serve with Senegalese rice (ceebu jën)
- Enjoy with hibiscus drink (bissap)
- Listen to West African rhythms
- Imagine strolling through Dakar's colorful streets while enjoying

1 person | 610 calories | 60 minutes

# South African Chicken Bunny Chow

South Africa's bunny chow is a flavorful surprise. Spiced chicken curry nestled inside a hollowed-out loaf of bread, a taste of Durban.

## Ingredients:

- 1 chicken thigh
- 1/4 cup chopped onion
- 2 cloves garlic
- 1/4 cup curry powder
- 1/4 cup chopped tomatoes
- Half loaf of bread

## Directions

1. Sauté onion and garlic.
2. Add curry powder and sear chicken.
3. Add tomatoes and simmer.
4. Hollow out bread and fill with chicken curry.
5. Savor the flavors of South Africa.

## Substitutions

- Serve with sambals (chutneys)
- Enjoy with South African rooibos tea
- Listen to Kwaito music
- Picture yourself at the Cape of Good Hope while enjoying

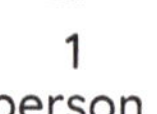

1 person

600 calories

90 minutes

# Ethiopian Doro Wat

Ethiopia's doro wat is a rich tapestry of flavors. Spiced chicken stew simmered with berbere, a taste of the Ethiopian highlands.

## Ingredients:

- 1 chicken leg quarter
- 1/4 cup chopped onion
- 2 cloves garlic
- 1/4 cup berbere spice blend
- 1/4 cup chopped tomatoes
- Injera bread for serving

## Directions

1. Sauté onion and garlic.
2. Add berbere and sear chicken.
3. Add tomatoes and simmer.
4. Serve with injera bread.
5. Immerse yourself in Ethiopian culture.

## Substitutions

- Niter kibbeh (spiced clarified butter) for authenticity
- Enjoy with Ethiopian coffee ceremony
- Listen to traditional Ethiopian music
- Imagine visiting Lalibela's rock-hewn churches while enjoying

1 person

590 calories

70 minutes

# Nigerian Jollof Rice with Chicken

Nigeria's jollof rice is a celebration of flavors. Spiced chicken and rice cooked in a tomato-based sauce, a taste of West African joy.

## Ingredients:

- 1 chicken thigh
- 1/4 cup chopped onion
- 2 cloves garlic
- 1/4 cup tomato paste
- 1/4 cup long-grain rice
- Fresh cilantro for garnish

## Directions

1. Sauté onion and garlic.
2. Add tomato paste and sear chicken.
3. Add rice and cook in sauce.
4. Garnish with cilantro.
5. Revel in Nigerian festivity.

## Substitutions

- Scotch bonnet pepper for extra heat
- Enjoy with Nigerian palm wine
- Listen to Afrobeat music
- Imagine dancing at Lagos' Ojuelegba intersection while enjoying

1
person

620
calories

80
minutes

# Moroccan Chicken Bastilla

Morocco's bastilla is a delicate masterpiece. Shredded chicken, fragrant spices, and toasted almonds wrapped in flaky pastry, a taste of elegance.

## Ingredients:

- 1 chicken thigh
- 1/4 cup chopped onion
- 2 cloves garlic
- 1/4 cup ground almonds
- 1/4 cup chopped fresh cilantro
- Phyllo pastry
- Powdered sugar and cinnamon for garnish

## Directions

1. Sauté onion and garlic.
2. Add ground almonds and sear chicken.
3. Add cilantro and spices.
4. Assemble bastilla with phyllo pastry.
5. Dust with sugar and cinnamon.
6. Indulge in Moroccan refinement.

## Substitutions

- Serve with Moroccan mint tea
- Listen to Andalusian music
- Imagine wandering through Marrakech's medina while enjoying

1 person | 580 calories | 70 minutes

# Tanzanian Chicken Pilau

Tanzania's pilau is a harmony of flavors. Spiced chicken rice pilaf infused with fragrant spices, a taste of East African allure.

## Ingredients:

- 1 chicken leg quarter
- 1/4 cup chopped onion
- 2 cloves garlic
- 1/4 cup basmati rice
- 1/4 tsp ground cumin
- 1/4 tsp ground cardamom
- Coconut milk for cooking

## Directions

1. Sauté onion and garlic.
2. Add rice, spices, and sear chicken.
3. Cook with coconut milk.
4. Delight in Tanzanian aromas.

## Substitutions

- Serve with kachumbari (tomato and onion salad)
- Listen to Swahili taarab music
- Imagine exploring Serengeti National Park while enjoying

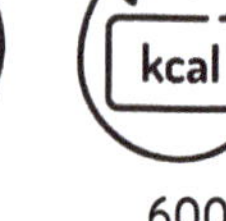

1 person | 600 calories | 80 minutes

# Sudanese Chicken Dama

Sudan's dama is a burst of flavors. Spiced chicken stew, slow-cooked with vegetables, a taste of Sahelian comfort.

## Ingredients:

- 1 chicken thigh
- 1/4 cup chopped onion
- 2 cloves garlic
- 1/4 cup chopped tomatoes
- 1/4 cup chopped bell peppers
- 1/4 cup chopped okra
- Dama sauce for cooking

## Directions

1. Sauté onion and garlic.
2. Add tomatoes, bell peppers, and sear chicken.
3. Cook with dama sauce and okra.
4. Experience Sudanese warmth.

## Substitutions

- Serve with Sudanese bread (kisra)
- Listen to Nubian music
- Imagine cruising down the Nile River while enjoying

1 person | 610 calories | 90 minutes

# Cameroonian Ndolé with Chicken

Cameroon's ndolé is a symphony of flavors. Chicken and bitter leaves stewed in a rich peanut sauce, a taste of Central African harmony.

## Ingredients:

- 1 chicken leg quarter
- 1/4 cup chopped onion
- 2 cloves garlic
- 1/4 cup ground peanuts
- 1/4 cup bitter leaves
- Palm oil for cooking

## Directions

1. Sauté onion and garlic.
2. Add ground peanuts and sear chicken.
3. Cook with palm oil and bitter leaves.
4. Relish in Cameroonian melodies.

## Substitutions

- Serve with plantains
- Listen to Makossa music
- Imagine trekking through Cameroon's rainforests while enjoying

1
person

590
calories

80
minutes

# Ghanaian Waakye with Chicken

Ghana's waakye is a symphony of colors and flavors. Rice and beans, infused with sorghum leaves, served with spicy chicken, a taste of West African vibrance.

## Ingredients:

- 1 chicken thigh
- 1/4 cup chopped onion
- 2 cloves garlic
- 1/4 cup tomato paste
- 1/4 cup cooked rice and beans mixture
- Shito sauce for serving

## Directions

1. Sauté onion and garlic.
2. Add tomato paste and sear chicken.
3. Serve chicken with waakye and shito sauce.
4. Celebrate Ghana's joy.

## Substitutions

- Serve with fried plantains
- Listen to Highlife music
- Imagine dancing at Accra's Makola Market while enjoying

1
person

580
calories

70
minutes

# Ivorian Kedjenou

Ivory Coast's kedjenou is a treasure of flavors. Chicken and vegetables slow-cooked in a clay pot, a taste of West African warmth.

## Ingredients:

- 1 chicken thigh
- 1/4 cup chopped onion
- 2 cloves garlic
- 1/4 cup chopped bell peppers
- 1/4 cup chopped eggplant
- 1/4 cup chopped tomato
- Kedjenou sauce for cooking

## Directions

1. Sauté onion and garlic.
2. Add bell peppers, eggplant, tomato, and sear chicken.
3. Cook with kedjenou sauce.
4. Bask in Ivorian coziness.

## Substitutions

- Serve with attiéké (cassava couscous)
- Listen to Coupe-Decale music
- Imagine strolling along Grand Bassam's beach while enjoying

# Chapter 6: Pacific and Island Delicacies

1
person

600
calories

80
minutes

# Fijian Chicken Curry

Fiji's chicken curry is a taste of paradise. Tender chicken simmered in fragrant spices and coconut milk, a journey to the South Pacific.

## Ingredients:

- 1 chicken thigh
- 1/4 cup chopped onion
- 2 cloves garlic
- 1/4 cup curry powder
- 1/4 cup coconut milk
- Chopped cilantro for garnish

## Directions

1. Sauté onion and garlic.
2. Add curry powder and sear chicken.
3. Add coconut milk and simmer.
4. Garnish with cilantro.
5. Immerse yourself in Fijian paradise.

## Substitutions

- Serve with taro root and cassava
- Listen to Fijian meke music
- Imagine lounging on Fiji's white sandy beaches while enjoying

1 person

590 calories

70 minutes

# Hawaiian Huli Huli Chicken

Hawaii's huli huli chicken is a taste of the islands. Grilled chicken marinated in a sweet and savory sauce, a tropical delight.

## Ingredients:

- 1 chicken leg quarter
- 1/4 cup pineapple juice
- 2 tbsp soy sauce
- 2 tbsp brown sugar
- 1/4 tsp ginger
- Sliced pineapple for serving

## Directions

1. Mix pineapple juice, soy sauce, brown sugar, and ginger.
2. Marinate chicken in mixture.
3. Grill until cooked.
4. Serve with grilled pineapple.
5. Revel in Hawaiian flavors.

## Substitutions

- Enjoy with a tropical fruit smoothie
- Listen to Hawaiian ukulele music
- Imagine catching waves on Waikiki Beach while enjoying

1 person

610 calories

90 minutes

# New Zealand Hangi Chicken

New Zealand's hangi chicken is a Maori tradition. Chicken and vegetables slow-cooked in an earth oven, a taste of Maori culture.

## Ingredients:

- 1 chicken thigh
- 1/4 cup chopped onion
- 2 cloves garlic
- 1/4 cup chopped kumara (sweet potato)
- 1/4 cup chopped cabbage
- Pounamu (greenstone) for serving

## Directions

1. Sauté onion and garlic.
2. Sear chicken and add vegetables.
3. Slow-cook in an earth oven.
4. Serve with pounamu for added significance.
5. Connect with Maori heritage.

## Substitutions

- Enjoy with Maori poi dance
- Listen to Maori waiata (songs)
- Imagine gazing at the Southern Cross constellation while enjoying

1 person | 600 calories | 80 minutes

# Samoan Oka with Chicken

Samoa's oka is a burst of island flavors. Raw fish salad with chicken, coconut cream, and citrus, a taste of Polynesian freshness.

## Ingredients:

- 1 chicken thigh
- 1/4 cup chopped onion
- 2 cloves garlic
- 1/4 cup coconut cream
- 1/4 cup lime juice
- Fresh mint for garnish

## Directions

1. Sauté onion and garlic.
2. Sear chicken and slice thinly.
3. Mix chicken with coconut cream and lime juice.
4. Garnish with fresh mint.
5. Dive into the essence of the Pacific.

## Substitutions

- Enjoy with a coconut water
- Listen to Polynesian drum beats
- Imagine swaying under the palm trees on a Samoan beach while enjoying

# Filipino Chicken Adobo with Pineapple

The Philippines' adobo gets a tropical twist. Chicken braised in soy-vinegar sauce with sweet pineapple, a taste of Filipino paradise.

## Ingredients:

- 1 chicken leg quarter
- 1/4 cup chopped onion
- 2 cloves garlic
- 1/4 cup soy sauce
- 1/4 cup vinegar
- Pineapple chunks for serving

## Directions

1. Sauté onion and garlic.
2. Add soy sauce and vinegar, sear chicken.
3. Simmer until chicken is tender.
4. Serve with pineapple chunks.
5. Enjoy the blend of sweet and savory in every bite.

## Substitutions

- Enjoy with a fresh buko (young coconut) juice
- Listen to Filipino folk songs
- Imagine watching the sunrise over Mayon Volcano while enjoying

# Chapter 7: Fusion and Modern Twists

1 person | 620 calories | 60 minutes

# Chicken Teriyaki Pizza

International fusion at its finest. A pizza with teriyaki chicken, melting cultures and flavors in every slice.

## Ingredients:

- 1 chicken breast
- 1/4 cup teriyaki sauce
- 1/4 cup mozzarella cheese
- Pizza dough
- Sliced bell peppers and red onion for topping

## Directions

1. Marinate chicken in teriyaki sauce and grill.
2. Spread teriyaki sauce on pizza dough.
3. Add chicken and toppings.
4. Sprinkle with cheese.
5. Bake until golden and melty.
6. Savor the global harmony.

## Substitutions

- Add a drizzle of sriracha for extra kick
- Experiment with other cheese varieties
- Imagine taking a culinary world tour while enjoying

1
person

590
calories

70
minutes

# Thai Green Curry Chicken Tacos

Fusion flavors collide in these Thai-inspired tacos. Spiced chicken green curry wrapped in a tortilla, a journey from Bangkok to Mexico.

## Ingredients:

- 1 chicken thigh
- 1/4 cup chopped onion
- 2 cloves garlic
- 1/4 cup Thai green curry paste
- 1/4 cup coconut milk
- Tortillas
- Fresh cilantro and lime wedges for garnish

## Directions

1. Sauté onion and garlic.
2. Add green curry paste and sear chicken.
3. Add coconut milk and simmer.
4. Serve in tortillas with cilantro and lime.
5. Embark on a global taco adventure.

## Substitutions

- Top with chopped peanuts for added crunch
- Add a dollop of Thai chili sauce for heat
- Imagine exploring the bustling streets of Bangkok while enjoying

1 person

600 calories

80 minutes

# Chicken Shawarma Burrito

The Middle East meets Mexico in this shawarma burrito. Spiced chicken wrapped in a tortilla, a fusion of flavors that will make your taste buds dance.

## Ingredients:

- 1 chicken thigh
- 1/4 cup chopped onion
- 2 cloves garlic
- 1/4 tsp cumin
- 1/4 tsp paprika
- Tortillas
- Sliced cucumber, tomato, and onion for topping

## Directions

1. Sauté onion and garlic.
2. Add cumin and paprika, sear chicken.
3. Slice chicken and assemble in tortillas with veggies.
4. Roll up and enjoy the fusion fiesta.

## Substitutions

- Add a drizzle of tahini or garlic sauce
- Experiment with different veggies and salsas
- Imagine wandering through the colorful souks of Marrakech while enjoying

1 person

590 calories

70 minutes

# Mango BBQ Chicken Sliders

Get ready for a slider sensation. Grilled mango BBQ chicken sliders, a modern twist that takes your taste buds on a flavor roller coaster.

## Ingredients:

- 1 chicken breast
- 1/4 cup mango BBQ sauce
- 1/4 cup coleslaw
- Slider buns
- Sliced avocado for topping

## Directions

1. Grill chicken and baste with mango BBQ sauce.
2. Toast slider buns.
3. Assemble sliders with chicken, coleslaw, and avocado.
4. Bite into the burst of flavors.

## Substitutions

- Add a slice of smoked gouda cheese for extra richness
- Experiment with different types of coleslaw
- Imagine picnicking in a tropical paradise while enjoying

1
person

610
calories

80
minutes

Ramen meets burger in this spicy delight. A ramen noodle bun with a juicy chicken patty, a fusion that will challenge your taste buds.

# Spicy Chicken Ramen Burger

## Ingredients:

- 1 chicken thigh
- 1/4 cup chopped onion
- 2 cloves garlic
- 1/4 tsp gochujang (Korean chili paste)
- Ramen noodle patty buns
- Sliced kimchi for topping

## Directions

1. Sauté onion and garlic.
2. Add gochujang and sear chicken.
3. Form ramen noodle patties and cook.
4. Assemble burgers with chicken and kimchi.
5. Experience a spicy and satisfying collision of flavors.

## Substitutions

- Add a fried egg for extra richness
- Experiment with different kimchi varieties
- Imagine strolling through Tokyo's bustling neighborhoods while enjoying

# We need your support

Reviews are hard to come by, and if you've been enjoying the recipes and content in this cookbook, we would be incredibly grateful if you could take a moment to show your support. Your feedback means the world to us and can make a significant difference for a small publisher like Garden of Grapes.

Here's how you can help:

1. Open the app or platform where you purchased this cookbook.
2. Find the "Review" or "Rating" button for the cookbook.
3. Give us a rating and a short sentence about your experience.

Your honest review can help us reach more readers and food enthusiasts, and it will mean a lot to our team. We read and appreciate every single review, and your support can have a positive impact on our future projects.

Thank you for being a part of our community and for considering leaving a review. Now, let's get back to exploring the wonderful world of recipes!

Happy cooking,
Alexander Jame Oliver and the Garden of Grapes Team

# Chapter 8: Exotic and Unique Creations

1 person | 610 calories | 80 minutes

# Maldivian Chicken Riha

Maldives' chicken riha is a taste of paradise in a bowl. Spiced chicken curry with coconut milk, a journey to the turquoise waters of the Indian Ocean.

## Ingredients:

- 1 chicken thigh
- 1/4 cup chopped onion
- 2 cloves garlic
- 1/4 tsp turmeric
- 1/4 tsp fenugreek seeds
- 1/4 cup coconut milk
- Fresh curry leaves for garnish

## Directions

1. Sauté onion and garlic.
2. Add turmeric and fenugreek seeds, sear chicken.
3. Add coconut milk and simmer.
4. Garnish with curry leaves.
5. Be transported to the tranquil Maldivian shores.

## Substitutions

- Serve with roshi (Maldivian flatbread)
- Listen to bodu beru drumming
- Imagine snorkeling among colorful coral reefs while enjoying

1
person

600
calories

70
minutes

# Cypriot Chicken Souvlaki Wrap

Cyprus' souvlaki wrap is a journey of flavors. Grilled chicken skewers wrapped in warm pita bread with tangy tzatziki, a taste of Mediterranean bliss.

## Ingredients:

- 1 chicken breast
- 1/4 cup chopped onion
- 2 cloves garlic
- 1/4 tsp oregano
- Pita bread
- Sliced tomatoes, cucumbers, and red onion
- Tzatziki sauce for serving

## Directions

1. Sauté onion and garlic.
2. Add oregano and grill chicken on skewers.
3. Warm pita bread and assemble with chicken, veggies, and tzatziki.
4. Revel in the Mediterranean symphony.

## Substitutions

- Add crumbled feta cheese for extra tang
- Experiment with different veggies in the wrap
- Imagine exploring the ancient ruins of Paphos while enjoying

1
person

610
calories

80
minutes

# Bhutanese Ema Datshi with Chicken

Bhutan's ema datshi gets a chicken twist. Spiced chicken stew with fiery chili and cheese, a taste of the Himalayas with a kick.

## Ingredients:

- 1 chicken thigh
- 1/4 cup chopped onion
- 2 cloves garlic
- 1/4 cup green chili peppers
- Bhutanese datshi cheese
- Red rice for serving

## Directions

1. Sauté onion and garlic.
2. Add green chili peppers and sear chicken.
3. Simmer with datshi cheese.
4. Serve with red rice.
5. Feel the Bhutanese mountain warmth.

## Substitutions

- Enjoy with suja (Bhutanese butter tea)
- Listen to Bhutanese folk music
- Imagine hiking to the Tiger's Nest Monastery while enjoying

1 person | 600 calories | 90 minutes

# Laotian Khao Piak Sen with Chicken

Laos' khao piak sen is a bowl of comfort. Chicken noodle soup with chewy rice noodles, a taste of Southeast Asian coziness.

## Ingredients:

- 1 chicken leg quarter
- 1/4 cup chopped onion
- 2 cloves garlic
- 1/4 cup rice flour
- Fresh herbs and lime wedges for garnish

## Directions

1. Sauté onion and garlic.
2. Sear chicken and simmer in broth.
3. Cook rice noodles and add to the broth.
4. Garnish with fresh herbs and lime.
5. Experience the serenity of Laos.

## Substitutions

- Add a dash of fish sauce for depth of flavor
- Enjoy with Lao iced coffee
- Imagine drifting down the Mekong River while enjoying

1
person

610
calories

70
minutes

# Montenegrin Chicken Ćevapi

Montenegro's ćevapi is a bite-sized delight. Grilled minced chicken sausages served with flatbread, a taste of Balkan comfort.

## Ingredients:

- Minced chicken
- 1/4 cup chopped onion
- 2 cloves garlic
- 1/4 tsp paprika
- Flatbread
- Ajvar (red pepper sauce) for serving

## Directions

1. Sauté onion and garlic.
2. Mix minced chicken with paprika.
3. Shape into sausages and grill.
4. Serve with flatbread and ajvar sauce.
5. Indulge in Balkan flavors.

## Substitutions

- Add chopped fresh parsley for freshness
- Enjoy with rakija (Balkan fruit brandy)
- Imagine strolling along Kotor's medieval streets while enjoying

# Chapter 9: Indigenous and Traditional

1 person | 620 calories | 80 minutes

# Inuit Akutaq with Chicken

The Arctic's akutaq is a taste of survival and tradition. Dried fish, berries, and chicken mixed into a hearty and unique creation.

## Ingredients:

- 1 chicken thigh
- 1/4 cup dried fish
- 2 tbsp rendered seal or whale fat
- Mixed berries
- Crushed nuts for texture

## Directions

1. Sauté chicken in rendered fat.
2. Combine with dried fish, berries, and nuts.
3. Enjoy a traditional Inuit dish that tells the story of survival.
4. Imagine the Arctic tundra while savoring.

## Substitutions

- Add a drizzle of agave nectar for sweetness
- Listen to Inuit throat singing
- Imagine the dancing Northern Lights while enjoying

1 person | 610 calories | 70 minutes

# Aboriginal Bush Tomato Chicken

Australia's bush tomato chicken is a taste of the outback. Chicken roasted with native bush tomatoes, a unique flavor journey through the Australian wilderness.

## Ingredients:

- 1 chicken thigh
- 1/4 cup chopped onion
- 2 cloves garlic
- 1/4 cup bush tomatoes
- Lemon myrtle leaves for seasoning

## Directions

1. Sauté onion and garlic.
2. Rub chicken with bush tomatoes and lemon myrtle.
3. Roast until cooked.
4. Savor the distinctive flavors of the Australian bush.

## Substitutions

- Enjoy with a cup of billy tea
- Listen to didgeridoo music
- Imagine hiking through the rugged Australian outback while enjoying

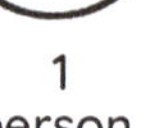

1 person | 600 calories | 80 minutes

# Native American Indian Fry Bread Taco

Native American fry bread taco is a canvas of flavors. Crispy fry bread topped with spiced chicken and traditional ingredients, a celebration of indigenous heritage.

## Ingredients:

- 1 chicken thigh
- 1/4 cup chopped onion
- 2 cloves garlic
- 1/4 tsp chili powder
- Fry bread
- Lettuce, tomato, and cheese for topping

## Directions

1. Sauté onion and garlic.
2. Add chili powder and sear chicken.
3. Assemble on fry bread with veggies and cheese.
4. Experience the connection to Native American culture.

## Substitutions

- Drizzle with honey for sweetness
- Listen to Native American flute music
- Imagine dancing at a powwow while enjoying

1
person

620
calories

90
minutes

# Maori Hangi Chicken

New Zealand's hangi chicken is a Maori tradition. Chicken and vegetables slow-cooked in an earth oven, a taste of Maori culture.

## Ingredients:

- 1 chicken thigh
- 1/4 cup chopped onion
- 2 cloves garlic
- 1/4 cup chopped kumara (sweet potato)
- 1/4 cup chopped cabbage
- Pounamu (greenstone) for serving

## Directions

1. Sauté onion and garlic.
2. Sear chicken and add vegetables.
3. Slow-cook in an earth oven.
4. Serve with pounamu for added significance.
5. Connect with Maori heritage.

## Substitutions

- Enjoy with Maori poi dance
- Listen to Maori waiata (songs)
- Imagine gazing at the Southern Cross constellation while enjoying

1 person | 600 calories | 80 minutes

# Amazonian Tucupi with Chicken

Brazil's tucupi with chicken is an Amazonian delight. Chicken stewed in tangy tucupi sauce, a taste of the lush rainforests and rivers of the Amazon.

## Ingredients:

- 1 chicken thigh
- 1/4 cup chopped onion
- 2 cloves garlic
- 1/4 cup tucupi sauce
- Cassava flour for thickening
- Fresh cilantro for garnish

## Directions

1. Sauté onion and garlic.
2. Add tucupi sauce and sear chicken.
3. Thicken with cassava flour.
4. Garnish with cilantro.
5. Immerse yourself in the Amazonian wilderness.

## Substitutions

- Serve with pirarucu fish and farinha (toasted manioc flour)
- Listen to Amazonian tribal music
- Imagine canoeing along the Amazon River while enjoying

# Chapter 10: Contemporary Gourmet

1 person | 630 calories | 40 minutes

# Truffle-infused Chicken Risotto

Indulge in luxury with truffle-infused chicken risotto. Creamy Arborio rice simmered with tender chicken and the earthy aroma of truffle, a gourmet delight.

## Ingredients:

- 1 chicken breast
- 1/4 cup Arborio rice
- 2 cups chicken broth
- 1/4 cup white wine
- Freshly shaved truffle
- Parmesan cheese for garnish

## Directions

1. Sear chicken and set aside.
2. Sauté Arborio rice in white wine.
3. Gradually add chicken broth and stir until creamy.
4. Slice chicken and serve on risotto.
5. Garnish with shaved truffle and Parmesan.
6. Elevate your culinary senses.

## Substitutions

- Drizzle with truffle oil for an extra layer of flavor
- Use porcini mushrooms instead of truffle
- Imagine dining in a Michelin-starred restaurant while enjoying

1 person | 580 calories | 30 minutes

# Lemon Herb Grilled Chicken Salad

A refreshing twist on salad. Grilled lemon herb chicken served over a bed of fresh greens with a zesty vinaigrette, a modern take on wholesome flavors.

## Ingredients:

- 1 chicken thigh
- Mixed salad greens
- Lemon herb marinade
- Zesty vinaigrette
- Fresh herbs for garnish

## Directions

1. Marinate chicken in lemon herb marinade.
2. Grill until cooked.
3. Toss salad greens with zesty vinaigrette.
4. Place grilled chicken on top.
5. Garnish with fresh herbs.
6. Enjoy a contemporary twist on classic salad.

## Substitutions

- Add crumbled goat cheese for creaminess
- Experiment with different greens and herbs
- Imagine picnicking in a sunlit garden while enjoying

1 person | 620 calories | 40 minutes

# Chicken and Mushroom Duxelles

Dine in elegance with chicken and mushroom duxelles. Chicken breast stuffed with savory mushroom duxelles, a refined blend of flavors and textures.

## Ingredients:

- 1 chicken breast
- 1/4 cup chopped mushrooms
- 2 cloves garlic
- Fresh thyme
- Creamy white wine sauce
- Sautéed spinach for serving

## Directions

1. Sauté mushrooms, garlic, and thyme for duxelles.
2. Stuff chicken breast with duxelles.
3. Grill until cooked.
4. Serve with creamy white wine sauce and sautéed spinach.
5. Revel in the symphony of refined tastes.

## Substitutions

- Add a slice of prosciutto for a salty touch
- Use a red wine reduction sauce for a bolder flavor
- Imagine dining in a luxurious chateau while enjoying

1 person | 630 calories | 35 minutes

# Black Garlic Butter Chicken

Elevate your senses with black garlic butter chicken. Pan-seared chicken drizzled with velvety black garlic butter, a contemporary masterpiece.

## Ingredients:

- 1 chicken thigh
- Black garlic butter
- Fresh herbs for garnish

## Directions

1. Sear chicken until golden.
2. Drizzle with black garlic butter.
3. Garnish with fresh herbs.
4. Savor the fusion of classic and modern flavors.

## Substitutions

- Serve with sautéed wild mushrooms for extra depth
- Experiment with different flavored butters
- Imagine dining in a chic urban bistro while enjoying

1
person

620
calories

45
minutes

# Smoked Paprika Roasted Chicken

Infuse smoky allure into your meal with smoked paprika roasted chicken. Juicy chicken with a tantalizing smoky flavor, a contemporary twist on comfort food.

## Ingredients:

- 1 chicken thigh
- Smoked paprika rub
- Roasted vegetables
- Chimichurri sauce for serving

## Directions

1. Rub chicken with smoked paprika.
2. Roast until cooked.
3. Serve with roasted vegetables and drizzle with chimichurri sauce.
4. Embrace the modern embrace of smoky goodness.

## Substitutions

- Add a sprinkle of chipotle pepper for extra heat
- Experiment with different roasted veggies
- Imagine enjoying dinner at a trendy rooftop restaurant while enjoying

# Chapter 11: Street Food Delights

1 person | 590 calories | 40 minutes

# Indian Chicken Kathi Roll

India's kathi roll is a burst of flavors in a wrap. Spiced chicken wrapped in a paratha with chutney and onions, a street food delight.

## Ingredients:

- 1 chicken thigh
- Spices for marinade
- Paratha
- Mint chutney, onions, and lemon wedges for serving

## Directions

1. Marinate chicken in spices.
2. Grill until cooked.
3. Warm paratha and assemble with chicken, chutney, onions, and lemon.
4. Relish the explosion of Indian street flavors.

## Substitutions

- Add sliced cucumber and tomato for freshness
- Experiment with different chutney flavors
- Imagine strolling through bustling Indian markets while enjoying

1 person

580 calories

35 minutes

# Mexican Tostadas with Chicken Tinga

Mexico's tostadas with chicken tinga are a fiesta in your mouth. Crispy tostadas topped with smoky chicken tinga, a celebration of vibrant Mexican flavors.

## Ingredients:

- 1 chicken thigh
- Chipotle peppers in adobo sauce
- Tostada shells
- Shredded lettuce, sour cream, and crumbled queso fresco for topping

## Directions

1. Shred chicken and mix with chipotle peppers.
2. Spread chicken tinga on tostada shells.
3. Top with lettuce, sour cream, and queso fresco.
4. Dive into the lively spirit of Mexican street food.

## Substitutions

- Add sliced avocado for creaminess
- Experiment with different toppings like pickled onions
- Imagine dancing to mariachi music in a bustling Mexican plaza while enjoying

1 person | 590 calories | 30 minutes

# Thai Basil Chicken Stir-Fry

Thailand's basil chicken stir-fry is a symphony of flavors. Spicy chicken cooked with fragrant Thai basil and served over steaming jasmine rice.

## Ingredients:

- 1 chicken thigh
- Thai basil leaves
- Fresh chili peppers
- Stir-fry sauce
- Jasmine rice for serving

## Directions

1. Sauté chicken with chili peppers.
2. Add Thai basil and stir-fry sauce.
3. Serve over jasmine rice.
4. Experience the harmonious blend of Thai aromas and heat.

## Substitutions

- Add a fried egg with a runny yolk for extra richness
- Experiment with different types of Thai chilies
- Imagine exploring bustling Bangkok markets while enjoying

1 person | 610 calories | 45 minutes

# Turkish Iskender Kebab with Chicken

Turkey's Iskender kebab with chicken is a culinary journey. Tender chicken on a bed of pita bread with tangy tomato sauce and creamy yogurt, a taste of Anatolian delight.

## Ingredients:

- 1 chicken thigh
- Pita bread
- Tomato sauce
- Yogurt
- Sumac and parsley for garnish

## Directions

1. Grill chicken until tender.
2. Warm pita bread and arrange chicken on top.
3. Drizzle with tomato sauce and yogurt.
4. Garnish with sumac and parsley.
5. Embark on a taste expedition through Turkey.

## Substitutions

- Add a dollop of pomegranate molasses for a sweet-tart touch
- Experiment with different yogurt varieties
- Imagine wandering through Istanbul's bustling streets while enjoying

1 person | 620 calories | 40 minutes

# Vietnamese Banh Mi with Grilled Chicken

Vietnam's banh mi with grilled chicken is a fusion of cultures. Crispy baguette filled with savory grilled chicken and vibrant Vietnamese flavors.

## Ingredients:

- 1 chicken thigh
- Baguette
- Pickled daikon and carrot
- Fresh cilantro and jalapeño slices for topping

## Directions

1. Grill chicken until charred and cooked.
2. Slice baguette and layer with chicken, pickled veggies, cilantro, and jalapeño.
3. Experience the harmonious blend of East and West in every bite.

## Substitutions

- Add a smear of pâté for richness
- Experiment with different types of baguette
- Imagine cruising through Halong Bay while savoring

# Chapter 12: Soul-Satisfying Stews

4 servings

380/se rving

30 mins

# French Coq au Vin Jaune

Legend has it that in Burgundy, France, a winemaker created this dish to celebrate a golden harvest. Chicken bathes in white wine, marrying with earthy mushrooms & herbs, warming hearts.

## Ingredients:

- 4 chicken thighs
- 2 cups white wine
- 1 cup chicken broth
- 200g mushrooms, quartered
- 1 onion, chopped
- 3 garlic cloves, minced
- 2 tbsp butter
- 2 tbsp olive oil
- 2 tbsp all-purpose flour
- 1 bouquet garni (thyme, parsley, bay leaves)
- Salt and pepper to taste

For Garnish:
- Fresh parsley, chopped

## Directions

1. In a Dutch oven, melt butter & olive oil. Brown chicken until golden. Remove & set aside.
2. Sauté onion, garlic & mushrooms.
3. Sprinkle flour, stir, add wine & broth. Add chicken back.
4. Toss in bouquet garni, season & simmer 20 mins.
5. Discard bouquet garni. Serve garnished with parsley.
6. Pair with a Burgundy white wine.

6
servings

420/se
rving

40
mins

# Mexican Pozole Verde with Chicken

In the heart of Mexico, Pozole Verde signifies celebration. A symphony of tender chicken and hominy dances in a vibrant green broth made from tomatillos, bringing life to any gathering.

## Ingredients:

- 1.5 lbs chicken breasts
- 2 cans hominy, drained
- 1 lb tomatillos, husked & boiled
- 2 poblano peppers
- 1 onion
- 3 garlic cloves
- 1 bunch cilantro
- 1 tbsp cumin
- 1 lime, juiced
- Salt and pepper to taste

For Garnish:

- Radishes, sliced
- Avocado, diced
- Tortilla chips
- Lime wedges

## Directions

1. Boil chicken until tender. Shred and set aside.
2. Blend tomatillos, poblanos, onion, garlic & cilantro.
3. Sauté mixture, add cumin, salt & pepper.
4. Add chicken, hominy & broth. Simmer 15 mins.
5. Stir in lime juice.
6. Serve with garnishes & tortilla chips for a festive touch.
7. Raise your bowl, shouting "¡Viva la vida!"

4 servings

320/serving

35 mins

# Caribbean Callaloo with Chicken

In the sun-soaked Caribbean, Callaloo whispers tales of rich history. Braised chicken finds its match in vibrant callaloo leaves, coconut milk, and island spices—a dance of flavors under the tropical moon.

## Ingredients:

- 4 chicken drumsticks
- 1 lb callaloo leaves, chopped
- 1 can coconut milk
- 1 onion, diced
- 2 tomatoes, chopped
- 3 garlic cloves, minced
- 1 Scotch bonnet pepper, whole
- 1 tsp thyme
- 1 tsp allspice
- Salt and pepper to taste

For Garnish:
- Lime wedges
- Sliced Scotch bonnet pepper

## Directions

1. Sear chicken until golden. Set aside.
2. Sauté onion, garlic & spices.
3. Add chicken, tomatoes & coconut milk. Simmer 15 mins.
4. Fold in callaloo leaves & Scotch bonnet pepper.
5. Simmer until leaves wilt.
6. Serve with rice & a squeeze of lime.
7. Feel the ocean breeze & let the rhythms of the Caribbean fill your soul.

6 servings | 480/serving | 50 mins

# Ghanaian Chicken Peanut Stew

In the heart of West Africa, comfort is found in Chicken Peanut Stew. Chicken swims in a velvety pool of peanuts, tomatoes, and spices, singing a song of unity and love across Ghanaian villages.

## Ingredients:

- 2 lbs chicken thighs
- 1 cup peanut butter
- 1 can diced tomatoes
- 2 onions, chopped
- 3 sweet potatoes, cubed
- 2 cups chicken broth
- 2 tbsp ginger, minced
- 2 tbsp curry powder
- 1 tsp cayenne pepper
- Salt and pepper to taste

For Garnish:
- Chopped peanuts
- Fresh cilantro, chopped

## Directions

1. Brown chicken, set aside.
2. Sauté onions, ginger & spices.
3. Stir in peanut butter, tomatoes & broth.
4. Add chicken & sweet potatoes. Simmer 25 mins.
5. Season with cayenne, salt & pepper.
6. Serve hot, garnished with peanuts & cilantro.
7. Taste the harmony of flavors—a gift from the vibrant land of Ghana.

4 servings | 420/serving | 45 mins

# Spanish Chicken and Chorizo Stew

In Spain's bustling kitchens, Chicken and Chorizo Stew captures the essence of the Iberian Peninsula. Chicken and spicy chorizo mingle with peppers and saffron, a celebration of Spanish fiestas.

## Ingredients:

- 4 chicken thighs
- 8 oz chorizo sausage, sliced
- 1 onion, diced
- 2 bell peppers, sliced
- 3 garlic cloves, minced
- 1 can diced tomatoes
- 1 cup chicken broth
- 1 tsp smoked paprika
- 1/2 tsp saffron threads
- Salt and pepper to taste

For Garnish:
- Fresh parsley, chopped
- Lemon wedges

## Directions

1. Brown chicken & chorizo. Set aside.
2. Sauté onion, peppers & garlic.
3. Add tomatoes, broth & spices. Simmer 20 mins.
4. Return chicken & chorizo. Simmer 10 mins.
5. Season with salt & pepper.
6. Serve garnished with parsley & a squeeze of lemon.
7. Close your eyes—taste the tapestry of Spain in every bite.

# Chapter 13: Rustic and Homestyle

5 servings

360/serving

50 mins

# Russian Chicken Kotleti

In the heart of Russia, Chicken Kotleti carries the whispers of grandmother's love. Minced chicken patties, kissed with herbs & fried golden, evoke memories of cozy dachas and endless family feasts.

## Ingredients:

- 1.5 lbs ground chicken
- 2 slices white bread, soaked in milk
- 1 onion, grated
- 2 eggs
- 1/4 cup fresh dill, chopped
- 1/4 cup fresh parsley, chopped
- 1/2 cup flour
- Salt and pepper to taste
- Oil for frying

For Serving:
- Sour cream
- Lingonberry jam

## Directions

1. Squeeze excess milk from bread. Mix with chicken, onion, eggs & herbs.
2. Form patties, coat with flour.
3. Fry until golden on both sides.
4. Serve hot with a dollop of sour cream & a spoonful of lingonberry jam.
5. Taste the flavors of a Russian childhood—where time stood still and love filled the air.

6
servings

440/se
rving

60
mins

# Amish Chicken Pot Pie

Nestled in the Amish heartland, Chicken Pot Pie tells tales of simplicity and warmth. Tender chicken and garden veggies snuggle in a flaky pastry, embodying the embrace of a close-knit community.

## Ingredients:

- 1.5 lbs chicken breasts
- 2 cups all-purpose flour
- 1/2 cup butter, cold & cubed
- 1 cup chicken broth
- 1 cup whole milk
- 2 carrots, diced
- 2 potatoes, diced
- 1 onion, chopped
- 1 cup frozen peas
- 1 tsp thyme
- Salt and pepper to taste

For Serving:
- Fresh parsley, chopped

## Directions

1. Boil chicken until cooked. Shred and set aside.
2. In a bowl, combine flour & butter to make dough. Roll out & line a pie dish.
3. Mix chicken, veggies, broth, milk & spices. Pour into pie crust.
4. Roll out another piece of dough for the top crust.
5. Bake until golden & bubbly.
6. Sprinkle parsley and dive into the comforting nostalgia of Amish kitchens.

4 servings | 380/serving | 55 mins

# Irish Chicken and Vegetable Casserole

Across Ireland's lush countryside, Chicken and Vegetable Casserole whispers tales of resilience. Chicken, hearty veggies & a creamy sauce unite in a casserole, embodying the spirit of Irish comfort.

## Ingredients:

- 4 chicken thighs
- 2 cups mixed vegetables (carrots, peas, corn)
- 1 onion, chopped
- 2 cloves garlic, minced
- 2 cups potatoes, sliced
- 1 cup chicken broth
- 1 cup heavy cream
- 2 tbsp butter
- 2 tbsp flour
- 1 tsp thyme
- Salt and pepper to taste

For Topping:
- Bread crumbs
- Chopped fresh parsley

## Directions

1. Brown chicken, set aside.
2. Sauté onion & garlic. Add veggies & thyme.
3. Make a roux with butter & flour, add broth & cream.
4. Layer chicken, veggies & sliced potatoes in a casserole dish.
5. Pour sauce over. Top with bread crumbs.
6. Bake until bubbly & golden.
7. Sprinkle parsley & let the Irish countryside embrace your senses.

4 servings

420/serving

40 mins

# Sri Lankan Chicken Kottu Roti

Sri Lanka's bustling streets resonate with the sizzle of Chicken Kottu Roti. Shredded godhamba roti, chicken, and an orchestra of spices dance on the griddle, narrating tales of island heritage.

## Ingredients:

- 2 cups shredded godhamba roti
- 1 lb chicken, cooked & shredded
- 1 onion, sliced
- 2 carrots, julienned
- 1 bell pepper, sliced
- 2 eggs
- 3 cloves garlic, minced
- 2 tbsp curry powder
- 1 tsp turmeric
- 1/2 tsp chili powder
- 1/2 cup leeks, chopped
- Salt and pepper to taste

For Serving:
- Lime wedges
- Chopped cilantro

## Directions

1. Heat oil, sauté onion & garlic. Add spices, followed by veggies & chicken.
2. Push aside, scramble eggs. Mix in roti.
3. Season with salt & pepper.
4. Serve hot, garnished with lime wedges & cilantro.
5. Close your eyes and let the bustling streets of Sri Lanka come alive on your palate.

6 servings | 400/serving | 70 mins

# Polish Chicken Kapusta

Deep in Poland's soul, Chicken Kapusta stirs memories of familial feasts. Chicken, sauerkraut & hearty Polish flavors simmer together, bridging the gap between tradition and comfort.

## Ingredients:

- 2 lbs chicken pieces
- 2 cups sauerkraut, drained
- 1 onion, chopped
- 2 apples, peeled & chopped
- 1/4 cup bacon, chopped
- 1/4 cup dried mushrooms, rehydrated & chopped
- 1 cup chicken broth
- 1 cup dry white wine
- 2 tbsp butter
- 2 tbsp flour
- 1 tsp caraway seeds
- Salt and pepper to taste

For Serving:
- Sour cream
- Chopped fresh dill

## Directions

1. Brown chicken & bacon. Set aside.
2. Sauté onion & mushrooms.
3. Add sauerkraut, apples & caraway seeds. Pour in broth & wine.
4. Return chicken to the pot. Simmer 45 mins.
5. Make a roux with butter & flour, add to the pot.
6. Season with salt & pepper.
7. Serve hot, topped with sour cream & dill.
8. Taste Poland's legacy—where history finds its place at the table.

# Chapter 14:
# Grilled and Barbecued Sensations

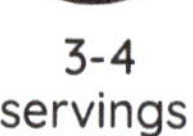

3-4 servings | 380/serving | 45 mins

# Korean Dak Galbi

In the heart of South Korea, Dak Galbi tells tales of vibrant flavors and communal dining. Marinated chicken, veggies & spicy gochujang sauce sizzle on a hot plate, igniting friendship and feasting.

## Ingredients:

- 1 lb chicken thighs, sliced
- 2 cups cabbage, sliced
- 1 cup sweet potatoes, thinly sliced
- 1 onion, sliced
- 2 scallions, chopped
- 1/4 cup gochujang (Korean red pepper paste)
- 3 tbsp soy sauce
- 2 tbsp sugar
- 1 tbsp minced garlic
- 1 tsp sesame oil
- 1 tsp sesame seeds
- Salt and pepper to taste

For Serving:
- Cooked rice
- Kimchi

## Directions

1. Marinate chicken in gochujang, soy sauce, sugar, garlic & sesame oil.
2. Heat a skillet, add chicken & veggies.
3. Stir-fry until cooked through.
4. Serve over rice, garnished with scallions & sesame seeds.
5. Share with friends, savoring the flavors that bridge cultures and create lasting memories.
6. "Annyeonghaseyo" to a new culinary adventure!

6
servings

420/se
rving

50
mins

# Southern BBQ Chicken

Deep in the heart of the American South, Southern BBQ Chicken tells the tale of smoky indulgence. Chicken, coated in tangy BBQ sauce, grills to perfection, embodying the essence of backyard gatherings.

## Ingredients:

- 2 lbs chicken pieces
- 2 cups BBQ sauce
- 1/4 cup brown sugar
- 1/4 cup apple cider vinegar
- 2 tsp smoked paprika
- 1 tsp garlic powder
- 1 tsp onion powder
- 1 tsp cayenne pepper
- Salt and pepper to taste

For Serving:
- Cornbread
- Coleslaw

## Directions

1. Mix BBQ sauce, sugar, vinegar & spices to make the marinade.
2. Coat chicken & marinate for a few hours.
3. Grill until cooked through, basting with extra sauce.
4. Serve hot, accompanied by cornbread & coleslaw.
5. Close your eyes and taste the smoky essence of Southern hospitality—where BBQ brings friends and family together.

4 servings

350/serving

40 mins

# Mongolian Chicken Kebabs

On the vast plains of Mongolia, Chicken Kebabs weave tales of nomadic flavors. Marinated chicken dances with soy, ginger & garlic, grilling to succulent perfection—a tribute to the open skies.

## Ingredients:

- 1.5 lbs chicken breasts, cubed
- 1/4 cup soy sauce
- 2 tbsp hoisin sauce
- 2 tbsp brown sugar
- 1 tbsp minced ginger
- 1 tbsp minced garlic
- 1 tbsp vegetable oil
- 1 tsp sesame oil
- 1 tsp sesame seeds
- Salt and pepper to taste

For Serving:
- Steamed rice
- Sliced green onions

## Directions

1. Mix soy sauce, hoisin, sugar, ginger, garlic & oils for marinade.
2. Coat chicken & marinate for 30 mins.
3. Thread onto skewers & grill until charred.
4. Sprinkle with sesame seeds.
5. Serve over rice, garnished with green onions.
6. Taste the freedom of the Mongolian steppes—a journey that speaks to the heart of ancient traditions.

4
servings

320/se
rving

55
mins

# Chilean Pebre Marinated Chicken

In Chile's colorful kitchens, Pebre Marinated Chicken whispers stories of vibrant heritage. Chicken bathed in pebre—a blend of fresh herbs, peppers & garlic—grills to perfection, celebrating the nation's zest for life.

## Ingredients:

- 4 chicken thighs
- 1 cup fresh cilantro, chopped
- 1/2 cup fresh parsley, chopped
- 1/4 cup olive oil
- 2 tbsp red wine vinegar
- 1 onion, diced
- 2 cloves garlic, minced
- 1 jalapeño, seeded & minced
- 1 tsp ground cumin
- Salt and pepper to taste

For Serving:
- Chilean pebre sauce
- Grilled corn

## Directions

1. Blend cilantro, parsley, oil, vinegar, onion, garlic, jalapeño & spices.
2. Marinate chicken for 30 mins to 1 hour.
3. Grill until cooked through & charred.
4. Serve with pebre sauce & grilled corn.
5. Close your eyes, let the vibrant colors of Chile dance on your plate, and savor the zest of South American life.

4 servings

380/serving

50 mins

# Egyptian Grilled Chicken Kofta

Amidst the history-laden streets of Egypt, Grilled Chicken Kofta spins tales of spice-laden streets. Ground chicken, aromatics & warm spices form kofta that sizzle on the grill, capturing the essence of ancient flavors.

## Ingredients:

- 1.5 lbs ground chicken
- 1 onion, grated
- 2 cloves garlic, minced
- 1/4 cup fresh parsley, chopped
- 1 tsp ground cumin
- 1 tsp ground coriander
- 1/2 tsp ground cinnamon
- 1/2 tsp ground nutmeg
- Salt and pepper to taste

For Serving:

- Pita bread
- Tzatziki sauce
- Sliced tomatoes
- Chopped mint

## Directions

1. Mix ground chicken, onion, garlic, herbs & spices.
2. Form kofta around skewers.
3. Grill until cooked & charred.
4. Serve in pita with tzatziki, tomatoes & mint.
5. Transport your taste buds to the land of pharaohs and spice-laden bazaars—an experience that transcends time.

# Chapter 15: Sweet and Savory Combinations

4
servings

400/se
rving

60
mins

# Apricot Glazed Chicken

## Ingredients:

- 4 chicken breasts
- 1 cup apricot preserves
- 1/4 cup soy sauce
- 2 tbsp Dijon mustard
- 2 tbsp brown sugar
- 1 tbsp apple cider vinegar
- 1 tsp minced ginger
- Salt and pepper to taste

For Serving:
- Roasted vegetables
- Fresh herbs

Across culinary borders, Apricot Glazed Chicken unfolds stories of harmony. Chicken, brushed with luscious apricot glaze & baked, creates a symphony of sweet and savory that transcends cultural boundaries.

## Directions

1. Mix apricot preserves, soy sauce, mustard, sugar, vinegar & ginger.
2. Season chicken, brush with glaze.
3. Bake until cooked through & glaze is caramelized.
4. Serve hot, accompanied by roasted veggies & herbs.
5. Taste the harmony of flavors—the way culinary borders can melt into one another, creating something beautifully unique.

4 servings | 360/serving | 50 mins

# Honey Mustard Chicken

Across lands, Honey Mustard Chicken narrates tales of balance. Chicken, coated in honey mustard glaze & baked to perfection, captures the essence of sweet and tangy coexistence.

## Ingredients:

- 4 chicken thighs
- 1/4 cup honey
- 1/4 cup Dijon mustard
- 2 tbsp whole grain mustard
- 2 tbsp olive oil
- 1 tbsp apple cider vinegar
- 1 tsp minced garlic
- Salt and pepper to taste

For Serving:
- Steamed green beans
- Mashed potatoes

## Directions

1. Mix honey, mustards, oil, vinegar & garlic for glaze.
2. Coat chicken, season.
3. Bake until golden & glazed.
4. Serve hot, with green beans & mashed potatoes.
5. Savor the sweet-tangy embrace—where flavors come together in a dance of perfect balance, much like life itself.

4 servings | 380/serving | 45 mins

# Pineapple Teriyaki Chicken

On the tropical breeze of international fusion, Pineapple Teriyaki Chicken sings stories of harmony. Chicken marinates in teriyaki & pineapple, grilling to perfection—a culinary bridge between lands.

## Ingredients:

- 4 chicken breasts
- 1 cup teriyaki sauce
- 1 cup pineapple juice
- 1/4 cup brown sugar
- 2 tbsp soy sauce
- 1 tbsp minced ginger
- 1 tbsp minced garlic
- Salt and pepper to taste

For Serving:
- Grilled pineapple slices
- Chopped green onions

## Directions

1. Mix teriyaki sauce, pineapple juice, sugar, soy sauce, ginger & garlic.
2. Marinate chicken for 30 mins to 1 hour.
3. Grill until cooked through, basting with marinade.
4. Serve with grilled pineapple & green onions.
5. Let the flavors whisk you away to a culinary paradise where oceans meet and cultures meld.

4
servings

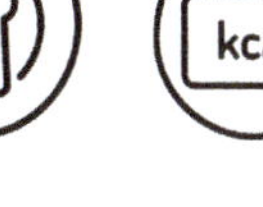

420/se
rving

55
mins

# Maple Bourbon Chicken

Through the amber-hued lens of Maple Bourbon Chicken, stories of warmth and comfort unfold. Chicken, glazed in maple bourbon sauce, roasts to perfection, celebrating the art of balance in flavors.

## Ingredients:

- 4 chicken thighs
- 1/4 cup maple syrup
- 1/4 cup bourbon
- 2 tbsp soy sauce
- 1 tbsp Dijon mustard
- 1 tsp minced garlic
- 1/2 tsp smoked paprika
- Salt and pepper to taste

For Serving:
- Roasted sweet potatoes
- Sauteed spinach

## Directions

1. Mix maple syrup, bourbon, soy sauce, mustard, garlic & paprika for glaze.
2. Coat chicken, season.
3. Roast until caramelized & cooked through.
4. Serve with sweet potatoes & spinach.
5. Let the flavors envelop you in a comforting embrace—a reminder that balance in life is as essential as balance on the plate.

4 servings | 380/serving | 50 mins

# Orange Ginger Chicken

Across the citrus groves, Orange Ginger Chicken weaves tales of zesty elegance. Chicken, marinated in orange & ginger, grills to perfection, reminding us that culinary brilliance often lies in simplicity.

## Ingredients:

- 4 chicken breasts
- 1/2 cup orange juice
- 1/4 cup soy sauce
- 2 tbsp honey
- 1 tbsp minced ginger
- 1 tsp minced garlic
- 1/2 tsp red pepper flakes
- Salt and pepper to taste

For Serving:
- Sliced oranges
- Chopped fresh cilantro

## Directions

1. Mix orange juice, soy sauce, honey, ginger, garlic & pepper flakes for marinade.
2. Marinate chicken for 30 mins to 1 hour.
3. Grill until cooked through, basting with marinade.
4. Serve with orange slices & cilantro.
5. Savor the zesty symphony—a reminder that sometimes, the most elegant melodies are composed of the simplest notes.

# Chapter 16: Comforting Classics

4 servings | 450/serving | 40 mins

# Creamy Chicken Alfredo

In the heart of Italy, Creamy Chicken Alfredo serenades with velvety elegance. Tender chicken, nestled in a rich Alfredo sauce, dances with fettuccine—a symphony of comfort that transcends borders.

## Ingredients:

- 1 lb chicken breasts
- 8 oz fettuccine
- 1 cup heavy cream
- 1/2 cup grated Parmesan cheese
- 1/4 cup butter
- 2 cloves garlic, minced
- 1/2 tsp nutmeg
- Salt and pepper to taste

For Serving:
- Chopped fresh parsley
- Additional Parmesan cheese

## Directions

1. Cook fettuccine until al dente. Set aside.
2. Season chicken & sauté until cooked through. Set aside.
3. In the same pan, melt butter & sauté garlic.
4. Pour in cream, Parmesan, nutmeg, salt & pepper.
5. Stir in cooked pasta & sliced chicken.
6. Serve hot, garnished with parsley & extra Parmesan.
7. Close your eyes, take a bite, and let the romance of Italy sweep you away.

6 servings | 380/serving | 60 mins

# Chicken and Dumplings

Across the United States, Chicken and Dumplings sings songs of nostalgia. Tender chicken, fluffy dumplings & a creamy broth unite, offering comfort that spans generations.

## Ingredients:

- 2 lbs chicken thighs
- 2 cups all-purpose flour
- 1/2 cup milk
- 1/4 cup butter
- 1 onion, chopped
- 2 carrots, diced
- 2 celery stalks, diced
- 2 cloves garlic, minced
- 4 cups chicken broth
- 1 cup heavy cream
- 1 tsp thyme
- Salt and pepper to taste

For Serving:
- Chopped fresh parsley

## Directions

1. Season chicken & sauté until golden. Set aside.
2. Make dumpling dough by mixing flour, milk & butter.
3. Sauté onion, carrots, celery & garlic.
4. Add broth, cream, thyme & chicken. Simmer 20 mins.
5. Drop spoonfuls of dumpling dough into the broth.
6. Cover & cook until dumplings are fluffy.
7. Serve hot, garnished with parsley.
8. Taste the essence of home—a reminder that comfort knows no boundaries.

4
servings

420/serving

50
mins

# Classic Chicken Curry

## Ingredients:

- 1.5 lbs chicken pieces
- 1 onion, chopped
- 2 tomatoes, chopped
- 1/2 cup plain yogurt
- 1/4 cup vegetable oil
- 2 cloves garlic, minced
- 1 tbsp minced ginger
- 1 tbsp curry powder
- 1 tsp ground turmeric
- 1 tsp ground cumin
- 1/2 tsp chili powder
- Salt and pepper to taste

For Serving:
- Cooked basmati rice
- Chopped fresh cilantro

Across the United Kingdom, Classic Chicken Curry tells tales of flavorful indulgence. Tender chicken simmers in aromatic spices, bathing in a curry sauce that transcends time and borders.

## Directions

1. Sauté onion, garlic & ginger in oil until fragrant.
2. Add spices, tomatoes & yogurt. Simmer until oil separates.
3. Add chicken & simmer until cooked through.
4. Season with salt & pepper.
5. Serve hot with basmati rice, garnished with cilantro.
6. Close your eyes, savor the flavors that span from the British Isles to the Indian subcontinent, and let the world unfold on your palate.

6 servings

400/serving

60 mins

# Chicken Pot Pie

Across the United States, Chicken Pot Pie whispers tales of comfort and tradition. Tender chicken, veggies & a flaky crust unite, offering a slice of nostalgia that knows no boundaries.

## Ingredients:

- 2 lbs chicken thighs
- 2 cups mixed vegetables (carrots, peas, corn)
- 1 onion, chopped
- 2 cloves garlic, minced
- 2 cups chicken broth
- 1 cup whole milk
- 1/4 cup butter
- 1/4 cup all-purpose flour
- 1 tsp thyme
- Salt and pepper to taste

For Crust:
- Store-bought pie crust
- Beaten egg (for egg wash)

## Directions

1. Boil chicken until cooked. Shred and set aside.
2. Sauté onion, garlic & veggies.
3. Make a roux with butter & flour, add broth & milk.
4. Add chicken, veggies & thyme. Simmer until thickened.
5. Pour mixture into a pie dish, cover with pie crust.
6. Brush crust with egg wash.
7. Bake until golden & bubbly.
8. Taste the timelessness of comfort—a reminder that a warm slice can bring smiles from coast to coast.

4
servings

360/se
rving

55
mins

# Homestyle Chicken and Rice Casserole

Across the world, Homestyle Chicken and Rice Casserole narrates tales of simplicity. Chicken, rice & veggies unite, baked to perfection—a testament that comfort knows no borders.

## Ingredients:

- 2 lbs chicken pieces
- 1 cup long-grain rice
- 2 cups chicken broth
- 1 onion, chopped
- 2 carrots, diced
- 1 cup frozen peas
- 1 cup frozen corn
- 1/2 cup milk
- 1/4 cup butter
- 1 tsp dried thyme
- Salt and pepper to taste

For Topping:
- Shredded cheddar cheese
- Bread crumbs

## Directions

1. Sauté onion & carrots in butter until softened.
2. Add rice & sauté briefly.
3. Pour in broth & milk, add chicken, peas, corn & thyme. Season.
4. Transfer to a baking dish, cover & bake until rice is cooked.
5. Top with cheese & breadcrumbs.
6. Broil until golden & bubbly.
7. Close your eyes, savor the flavors—the embrace of home that transcends oceans and cultures.

# Chapter 17: Hearty and Wholesome

4
servings

360/serving

50
mins

# Mediterranean Chicken with Olives and Tomatoes

Amidst the sun-soaked Mediterranean, Chicken with Olives and Tomatoes tells tales of wholesome indulgence. Chicken, olives & tomatoes bask in olive oil & herbs, offering a taste of the Mediterranean diet.

## Ingredients:

- 4 chicken breasts
- 1 cup cherry tomatoes
- 1/2 cup Kalamata olives, pitted
- 1/4 cup olive oil
- 2 cloves garlic, minced
- 1 tsp dried oregano
- 1 tsp dried thyme
- Salt and pepper to taste

For Serving:
- Crumbled feta cheese
- Chopped fresh parsley

## Directions

1. Season chicken & sauté until golden. Set aside.
2. In the same pan, sauté garlic until fragrant.
3. Add tomatoes & olives. Cook until tomatoes burst.
4. Return chicken to the pan.
5. Drizzle with olive oil, sprinkle with herbs, salt & pepper.
6. Bake until chicken is cooked through.
7. Serve hot, garnished with feta & parsley.
8. Let the flavors of the Mediterranean whisk you away to azure waters and ancient cities.

4 servings

420/serving

45 mins

# Middle Eastern Chicken Shawarma Bowl

Across the Middle East, Chicken Shawarma Bowl spins tales of bold flavors. Marinated chicken, fragrant spices & colorful veggies unite in a bowl—a culinary journey that spans from the Levant to your plate.

## Ingredients:

- 1.5 lbs chicken thighs, sliced
- 1 cup plain yogurt
- 2 tbsp olive oil
- 2 cloves garlic, minced
- 1 tsp ground cumin
- 1 tsp ground paprika
- 1/2 tsp ground turmeric
- 1/2 tsp ground cinnamon
- Salt and pepper to taste

For Serving:
- Cooked couscous
- Chopped fresh mint

## Directions

1. Mix yogurt, oil, garlic & spices for marinade.
2. Coat chicken & marinate for 1-2 hours.
3. Sauté chicken until cooked through.
4. Serve over couscous, garnished with mint.
5. Taste the flavors of the Middle East—where spices tell stories that date back centuries, and where each bite is a step into a vibrant market.

4 servings

380/serving

40 mins

# Thai Coconut Chicken Soup (Tom Kha Gai)

Amidst Thailand's aromatic kitchens, Tom Kha Gai whispers tales of soothing delight. Chicken, mushrooms & coconut milk dance in a fragrant broth, a warm embrace for the senses.

## Ingredients:

- 1 lb chicken thighs, sliced
- 1 can (13.5 oz) coconut milk
- 4 cups chicken broth
- 1 cup sliced mushrooms
- 2 stalks lemongrass, bruised
- 3 kaffir lime leaves
- 2 tbsp fish sauce
- 1 tbsp minced galangal
- 1 tbsp lime juice
- 2 Thai chilies, sliced
- Salt and pepper to taste

For Serving:
- Chopped fresh cilantro
- Sliced green onions

## Directions

1. In a pot, bring coconut milk & chicken broth to a simmer.
2. Add lemongrass, lime leaves, galangal & chicken. Simmer until chicken is cooked through.
3. Stir in mushrooms, fish sauce, lime juice & chilies.
4. Season with salt & pepper.
5. Serve hot, garnished with cilantro & green onions.
6. Let the aroma of Thai herbs and coconut fill the air, and transport yourself to the land of smiles.

6
servings

360/se
rving

55
mins

# Mexican Chicken Tortilla Soup

Amidst the vibrant colors of Mexico, Chicken Tortilla Soup narrates tales of zestful comfort. Chicken, veggies & tortilla strips dance in a spicy tomato broth—a symphony that celebrates the heart of Mexican cuisine.

## Ingredients:

- 2 lbs chicken breasts
- 1 can (14 oz) diced tomatoes
- 1 onion, chopped
- 2 cloves garlic, minced
- 1 jalapeño, chopped
- 1 cup corn kernels
- 1 cup black beans, drained
- 1 tsp ground cumin
- 1 tsp chili powder
- 1/2 tsp smoked paprika
- Salt and pepper to taste

For Serving:
- Crushed tortilla chips
- Sliced avocado
- Chopped fresh cilantro

## Directions

1. Sauté onion, garlic & jalapeño until softened.
2. Add tomatoes, spices, chicken & broth. Simmer until chicken is cooked.
3. Shred chicken & return to the pot with corn & beans.
4. Season with salt & pepper.
5. Serve hot, garnished with tortilla chips, avocado & cilantro.
6. Taste the vibrancy of Mexico—where every spoonful is a fiesta for the senses.

6
servings

340/se
rving

60
mins

# Indian Chicken Mulligatawny Soup

Amidst the spice-laden markets of India, Chicken Mulligatawny Soup weaves tales of complexity. Chicken, lentils & aromatic spices simmer in a rich broth—a journey that captures the essence of Indian cuisine.

## Ingredients:

- 1 lb chicken thighs, cubed
- 1 cup red lentils
- 2 carrots, diced
- 1 onion, chopped
- 2 cloves garlic, minced
- 1 apple, peeled & chopped
- 2 tsp curry powder
- 1 tsp ground turmeric
- 1/2 tsp ground cumin
- 1/2 tsp ground coriander
- Salt and pepper to taste

For Serving:
- Chopped fresh cilantro
- Sliced lime

## Directions

1. Sauté onion, garlic & carrots until softened.
2. Add spices & sauté briefly.
3. Add chicken, lentils & broth. Simmer until chicken is cooked.
4. Stir in chopped apple.
5. Season with salt & pepper.
6. Serve hot, garnished with cilantro & lime.
7. Embark on a culinary journey to India, where every bite is a symphony of spices, colors, and stories that date back millennia.

# Chapter 18: Vibrant Salads

4 servings | 320/serving | 40 mins

# Greek Chicken Souvlaki Salad

Amidst the sun-soaked landscapes of Greece, Chicken Souvlaki Salad sings songs of freshness. Marinated chicken, crisp veggies & tangy feta dance in harmony—a taste of the Mediterranean on your plate.

## Ingredients:

- 1.5 lbs chicken breasts
- 1 cucumber, sliced
- 1 cup cherry tomatoes, halved
- 1/2 red onion, thinly sliced
- 1/2 cup Kalamata olives, pitted
- 1/4 cup crumbled feta cheese
- 2 tbsp olive oil
- 2 tbsp lemon juice
- 1 tsp dried oregano
- Salt and pepper to taste

For Serving:
- Pita bread
- Tzatziki sauce
- Chopped fresh parsley

## Directions

1. Mix olive oil, lemon juice, oregano, salt & pepper for marinade.
2. Coat chicken & marinate for 30 mins.
3. Grill until cooked through & charred.
4. Slice chicken and assemble salad with veggies, olives & feta.
5. Drizzle with more olive oil & lemon juice.
6. Serve with pita & tzatziki, garnished with parsley.
7. Close your eyes, take a bite, and let the beauty of Greece envelop you.

4
servings

360/se
rving

45
mins

# Mexican Grilled Chicken Salad with Avocado

Amidst the vibrant markets of Mexico, Grilled Chicken Salad with Avocado narrates tales of zest. Chicken, black beans & avocado unite in a colorful fiesta—a celebration of flavors that dance on your taste buds.

## Ingredients:

- 1.5 lbs chicken thighs
- 1 cup black beans, drained
- 1 avocado, sliced
- 1 cup corn kernels
- 1 cup cherry tomatoes, halved
- 1/4 cup chopped red onion
- 1/4 cup chopped fresh cilantro
- 2 tbsp lime juice
- 2 tbsp olive oil
- 1 tsp ground cumin
- Salt and pepper to taste

For Serving:
- Tortilla strips
- Lime wedges
- Sliced jalapeños

## Directions

1. Mix olive oil, lime juice, cumin, salt & pepper for marinade.
2. Coat chicken & marinate for 30 mins.
3. Grill until cooked through & charred.
4. Assemble salad with black beans, avocado, corn, tomatoes & onion.
5. Drizzle with more olive oil & lime juice.
6. Garnish with cilantro, tortilla strips, lime wedges & jalapeños.
7. Taste the vibrancy of Mexico—where each bite is a fiesta for your senses.

4 servings | 340/serving | 50 mins

# Middle Eastern Fattoush Salad with Grilled Chicken

Amidst the bustling bazaars of the Middle East, Fattoush Salad with Grilled Chicken weaves tales of freshness. Chicken, crispy pita & vibrant veggies unite in a medley of flavors—a culinary journey across the Levant.

## Ingredients:

- 1.5 lbs chicken breasts
- 4 pita breads, torn into pieces
- 2 cups chopped romaine lettuce
- 1 cup cucumber, diced
- 1 cup cherry tomatoes, halved
- 1/2 red onion, thinly sliced
- 1/4 cup chopped fresh parsley
- 1/4 cup chopped fresh mint
- 2 tbsp olive oil
- 2 tbsp lemon juice
- 1 tsp sumac
- Salt and pepper to taste

For Serving:
- Crumbled feta cheese
- Lemon wedges

## Directions

1. Mix olive oil, lemon juice, sumac, salt & pepper for marinade.
2. Coat chicken & marinate for 30 mins.
3. Grill until cooked through & charred.
4. Toast pita until crispy.
5. Assemble salad with lettuce, cucumber, tomatoes, onion, parsley & mint.
6. Drizzle with more olive oil & lemon juice.
7. Top with chicken, pita & feta, and garnish with sumac.
8. Let the flavors of the Middle East dance on your palate—a tribute to ancient traditions.

4
servings

320/se
rving

40
mins

# Thai Larb Gai Salad

Amidst the aromatic streets of Thailand, Larb Gai Salad whispers tales of bold flavors. Minced chicken, fragrant herbs & zesty lime unite in a dish that's a burst of Southeast Asian delight.

## Ingredients:

- 1.5 lbs ground chicken
- 1 cup chopped fresh mint
- 1/2 cup chopped fresh cilantro
- 1/4 cup chopped red onion
- 2 tbsp fish sauce
- 2 tbsp lime juice
- 1 tbsp ground chili flakes
- 1 tbsp toasted rice powder
- 1 tsp sugar
- Salt to taste

For Serving:
- Lettuce leaves
- Sliced cucumbers
- Chopped peanuts
- Lime wedges
- Thai chili slices

## Directions

1. Cook ground chicken until no longer pink. Set aside.
2. In a bowl, mix fish sauce, lime juice, chili flakes, sugar & salt.
3. Toss chicken with the sauce & toasted rice powder.
4. Add mint, cilantro & onion, and toss gently.
5. Serve on lettuce leaves, garnished with cucumber, peanuts, lime wedges & chili slices.
6. Taste the boldness of Thailand—where each bite is a symphony of herbs and spices.

4 servings | 380/serving | 35 mins

# Caesar Salad with Grilled Chicken

Amidst the elegance of international dining, Caesar Salad with Grilled Chicken narrates tales of timeless taste. Grilled chicken, crisp romaine & tangy dressing unite—a culinary classic that transcends cultures.

## Ingredients:

- 1.5 lbs chicken breasts
- 2 heads romaine lettuce, torn
- 1 cup croutons
- 1/2 cup grated Parmesan cheese
- 1/4 cup Caesar dressing
- 2 tbsp olive oil
- 2 cloves garlic, minced
- Salt and pepper to taste

For Serving:
- Lemon wedges

## Directions

1. Mix olive oil, garlic, salt & pepper for marinade.
2. Coat chicken & grill until cooked through & charred.
3. Assemble salad with romaine, croutons & Parmesan.
4. Drizzle with Caesar dressing.
5. Top with sliced grilled chicken.
6. Squeeze lemon over the salad before serving.
7. Experience the timeless allure of Caesar—a culinary masterpiece that's a favorite around the world.

# Chapter 19: Global Noodle Dishes

4
servings

380/se
rving

45
mins

# Chinese Chicken Chow Mein

Amidst the bustling streets of China, Chicken Chow Mein spins tales of wok-tossed delight. Chicken, veggies & stir-fried noodles unite—a symphony of flavors that's a testament to Chinese culinary artistry.

## Ingredients:

- 1.5 lbs chicken breasts, sliced
- 8 oz chow mein noodles
- 2 cups sliced mixed vegetables (bell peppers, carrots, snow peas)
- 1/4 cup oyster sauce
- 2 tbsp soy sauce
- 2 tbsp hoisin sauce
- 2 cloves garlic, minced
- 1 tsp minced ginger
- 2 tbsp vegetable oil
- Salt and pepper to taste

For Serving:
- Chopped green onions

## Directions

1. Cook chow mein noodles according to package instructions. Set aside.
2. Season chicken with salt & pepper.
3. Heat oil in a wok, stir-fry chicken until cooked. Set aside.
4. In the same wok, stir-fry garlic, ginger & veggies.
5. Add chicken, noodles, oyster sauce, soy sauce & hoisin sauce.
6. Toss until heated through.
7. Serve hot, garnished with green onions.
8. Taste the essence of Chinese street food—a dance of flavors that's as captivating as it is delicious.

4 servings

420/serving

35 mins

# Italian Chicken Fettuccine Alfredo

Amidst the romantic settings of Italy, Chicken Fettuccine Alfredo whispers tales of creamy elegance. Grilled chicken, al dente pasta & velvety Alfredo sauce unite—a dish that's as comforting as a gondola ride along the canals of Venice.

## Ingredients:

- 1.5 lbs chicken breasts
- 8 oz fettuccine pasta
- 1 cup heavy cream
- 1/2 cup grated Parmesan cheese
- 1/4 cup butter
- 2 cloves garlic, minced
- 1 tsp dried parsley
- Salt and pepper to taste

For Serving:
- Chopped fresh parsley
- Additional grated Parmesan cheese

## Directions

1. Cook fettuccine until al dente. Set aside.
2. Season chicken with salt & pepper.
3. Grill until cooked through & charred.
4. In a saucepan, melt butter & sauté garlic.
5. Pour in cream, add Parmesan, dried parsley, salt & pepper.
6. Toss cooked fettuccine in the sauce.
7. Slice grilled chicken and serve on top of the pasta.
8. Garnish with fresh parsley & extra Parmesan.
9. Let the flavors of Italy sweep you away—a culinary journey that's amore in every bite.

4
servings

360/se
rving

50
mins

# Japanese Chicken Ramen

Amidst the bustling ramen shops of Japan, Chicken Ramen tells tales of umami goodness. Chicken, noodles & savory broth unite in a bowl —a tribute to the soul-warming comfort of Japanese cuisine.

## Ingredients:

- 1.5 lbs chicken thighs
- 8 oz ramen noodles
- 4 cups chicken broth
- 2 cups water
- 1 cup sliced mushrooms
- 2 boiled eggs, halved
- 1/4 cup soy sauce
- 2 cloves garlic, minced
- 1 tsp minced ginger
- 1 tsp sesame oil
- Salt and pepper to taste

For Serving:
- Sliced green onions
- Nori seaweed sheets
- Toasted sesame seeds

## Directions

1. Season chicken with salt & pepper.
2. Grill until cooked through & charred.
3. In a pot, bring chicken broth, water, soy sauce, garlic & ginger to a simmer.
4. Add sliced mushrooms & sesame oil.
5. Cook ramen noodles according to package instructions.
6. Assemble bowls with noodles, broth, sliced chicken & halved eggs.
7. Garnish with green onions, nori & sesame seeds.
8. Taste the flavors of Japan—where every slurp is a tribute to tradition and craftsmanship.

4 servings | 340/serving | 55 mins

# Malaysian Chicken Laksa

Amidst the vibrant hawker stalls of Malaysia, Chicken Laksa narrates tales of spicy indulgence. Chicken, rice noodles & aromatic broth unite—a symphony of flavors that captures the essence of Southeast Asian street food.

## Ingredients:

- 1.5 lbs chicken breasts
- 8 oz rice noodles
- 4 cups chicken broth
- 1 can (14 oz) coconut milk
- 1 cup sliced mixed vegetables (bean sprouts, bok choy)
- 1/4 cup laksa paste
- 2 tbsp vegetable oil
- 1 tbsp fish sauce
- 1 tbsp lime juice
- 1 tsp sugar
- Salt and pepper to taste

For Serving:
- Chopped fresh cilantro
- Sliced red chili
- Lime wedges

## Directions

1. Season chicken with salt & pepper.
2. Grill until cooked through & charred.
3. In a pot, sauté laksa paste in oil until fragrant.
4. Add chicken broth & coconut milk. Simmer.
5. Stir in fish sauce, lime juice, sugar, salt & pepper.
6. Cook rice noodles according to package instructions.
7. Assemble bowls with noodles, broth, sliced chicken & mixed vegetables.
8. Garnish with cilantro, chili & lime wedges.
9. Embark on a culinary journey to Malaysia—where each spoonful is an explosion of flavors and cultures.

4
servings

400/se
rving

60
mins

# Turkish Chicken İskender Noodles

Amidst the bustling bazaars of Turkey, Chicken İskender Noodles sings songs of indulgence. Grilled chicken, buttery bread & savory tomato sauce unite—a culinary masterpiece that's a tribute to the grandeur of Turkish cuisine.

## Ingredients:

- 1.5 lbs chicken thighs
- 8 oz egg noodles
- 1 cup tomato sauce
- 1/2 cup plain yogurt
- 1/4 cup butter
- 1/4 cup olive oil
- 2 cloves garlic, minced
- 1 tsp ground paprika
- Salt and pepper to taste

For Serving:
- Sliced pide bread (Turkish flatbread)
- Chopped fresh parsley
- Melted butter

## Directions

1. Season chicken with salt & pepper.
2. Grill until cooked through & charred.
3. Cook egg noodles until al dente. Set aside.
4. In a saucepan, melt butter & sauté garlic & paprika.
5. Add tomato sauce & simmer.
6. Assemble bowls with noodles & sliced chicken.
7. Drizzle tomato sauce over the chicken.
8. Serve with yogurt, sliced pide bread & parsley.
9. Indulge in the opulence of Turkey—where history and flavor meld into an unforgettable experience.

# We need your support

Enjoyed the Cookbook? Share Your Thoughts!

As you come to the end of this culinary journey, we sincerely hope you've found inspiration, delicious recipes, and a touch of joy within the pages of this cookbook. Crafting these recipes and sharing them with you has been a labor of love, and we'd be immensely grateful if you could spare a moment to leave us a review.

Reviews are a lifeline for small publishers like us, and your feedback can make a significant impact:

1. Navigate back to the app or platform where you purchased this cookbook.
2. Look for the "Review" or "Rating" option associated with the cookbook.
3. Rate your experience and share a brief sentence about what you enjoyed.

Your honest review can help us reach more fellow food enthusiasts, allowing us to continue creating and sharing culinary magic. We understand that reviews can be rare gems, but each one holds immeasurable value for us.

We truly appreciate your support, understanding, and the time you've invested in exploring our recipes. Your feedback guides us and brings us closer to our goal of providing you with exceptional culinary experiences. Please remember that while we strive for perfection, a few typos or minor hiccups may have slipped through. Your kindness and understanding mean the world to us.

Thank you for being a part of the Garden of Grapes community. Your review can transform our journey, and we eagerly anticipate hearing your thoughts.

With heartfelt gratitude,
Alexander Jame Oliver and the Garden of Grapes Team

www.ingramcontent.com/pod-product-compliance
Ingram Content Group UK Ltd.
Pitfield, Milton Keynes, MK11 3LW, UK
UKHW050146280726
14058UKWH00007B/852

9 798869 178596